GroupBuilder™ Games and Activities for Youth Ministry

Loveland, Colorado

CONTRIBUTORS

We'd like to thank the following people,
who contributed their creative ideas and hard work to this collection.

Michael W. Capps
Karen Dockrey
Monica Kay Glenn
Debbie Gowensmith
Stacy L. Haverstock
Michele Howe
Jan Kershner
Trish Kline

Jim Kochenburger
Pamela Malloy
Kelly Martin
Marilyn Meiklejohn
Janet Dodge Narum
Todd Outcalt
Christina Schofield
Cheryl Slater

GROUPBUILDER™ GAMES AND ACTIVITIES FOR YOUTH MINISTRY

Copyright © 2000 Group Publishing, Inc.

Visit our Web site: **www.group.com**

Credits
Editor: Julie Meiklejohn
Senior Editor: Jim Kochenburger
Chief Creative Officer: Joani Schultz
Copy Editor: Stephen Beal
Art Director: Kari K. Monson
Cover Art Director: Jeff A. Storm
Cover Designer: Alan Furst, Inc.
Computer Graphic Artist: Andrea Reider
Cover Illustrator: Scott Matthews
Illustrator: Dave Klug
Production Manager: Alexander Jorgensen

Unless otherwise noted, Scripture taken from the HOLY BIBLE, NEW INTERNATIONAL VERSION®. Copyright © 1973, 1978, 1984 by International Bible Society. Used by permission of Zondervan Publishing House. All rights reserved.

Library of Congress Cataloging-in-Publication Data
GroupBuilder games and activities for youth ministry.
    p. cm.
  ISBN 0-7644-2197-2 (alk. paper)
   1. Church group work with youth. 2. Christian education--Activity programs. I. Title:
Games and activities for youth ministry. II. Group Publishing.

BV4447 .G6943 2000
268'.433--dc21
                                                               00-026423

10 9 8 7 6   09 08 07 06 05
Printed in the United States of America.

Contents

introduction   4

relationship builders   6

trust builders   33

unity builders   51

confidence builders   73

faith builders   95

Introduction

A youth group is an amazing organism. Where else can you see the quarterback for the high school football team, the future valedictorian, and a skater worship and grow together? Church is a place where teenagers can leave their differences at the door and come together in Jesus' holy name. And this is exactly what Christians have been called to do.

However, bringing teenagers together may not always be so easy. The differences between them sometimes lead them to overlook their similarities. They may find it difficult to communicate with each other when it seems, because of different interests or backgrounds, that they're not even speaking the same language. What's needed are ways to bring these diverse young people together, and to have some fun along the way.

So provide some fun and common ground for your teenagers—and you can do it with this book! Two of the biggest reasons teenagers come to youth group are 1) to hang out with their friends and 2) to have fun. The games in this book provide countless opportunities to meet both needs; they also fulfill teenagers' deeper, often unspoken need for spiritual nourishment and guidance. These games can also help teenagers build strong bonds with one another, regardless of any differences that may keep them apart outside church walls.

GroupBuilder™ Games and Activities for Youth Ministry is divided into five sections, each designed to meet different needs within your group.

The "Relationship Builders" section encourages teenagers to get to know each other better and begin to form lasting relationships with each other. The games focus on both group and one-on-one relationships.

Teenagers often have a difficult time trusting each other. The "Trust Builders" section provides many different exercises to help teenagers open themselves up and trust one another more.

The "Unity Builders" section helps the group become a more cohesive unit through shared experiences. Teenagers will work together and rely on each other in these games.

The games in the "Confidence Builders" section build up individuals and encourage them to build up each other. These games will help teenagers gain personal and social confidence within the group.

Finally, the games in the "Faith Builders" section help teenagers grow in their faith and their relationship with Jesus.

Many of the games in *GroupBuilder™ Games and Activities for Youth Ministry* will help teenagers to laugh and have a good time. The games will also provide fresh new insights through discussion and debriefing experiences. The combination will serve to bond the members of your group as they follow Jesus.

"I urge you to live a life worthy of the calling you have received. Be completely humble and gentle; be patient, bearing with one another in love. Make every effort to keep the unity of the Spirit through the bond of peace. There is one body and one Spirit...one Lord, one faith, one baptism; one God and Father of all" (Ephesians 4:1b-6a).

Relationship Builders

The Envelope, Please

OVERVIEW: Teenagers will guess information about each other to learn how well they actually know each other.

TIME INVOLVED: 10 to 15 minutes

SUPPLIES: marker, legal envelopes, index cards, pencils, paper

PREPARATION: With a marker, write a consecutive number on an envelope for each member of the group. Then shuffle the envelopes.

Give each teenager one envelope. Tell them to place their envelopes face down so the numbers aren't visible. Then give each person an index card and a pencil.

Say: **I'd like you to write one statement about yourself on your index card. One example of a suitable statement is "I'm great at math, and I'll probably be a rocket scientist some day." When you're finished, put the card in your envelope and make a mental note of the number on the front. Then give your envelope to me.**

When you've received all the envelopes, give each teenager a sheet of paper. Have them write the consecutive numbers down one side of their papers. While they do this, put the envelopes in order.

Take the cards from the envelopes one by one. Give the number on each envelope, and then read each statement aloud. Have the group guess whose statement it is by writing that person's name beside the number you have given.

When you've read all the cards, go down the list together and have group members identify which facts were theirs.

Lead a short discussion. Ask:

• **Why was it difficult in some cases to guess who wrote these statements?**

• **How is this like or unlike drawing conclusions about one another based on a few facts?**

• **What is the problem with judging or making conclusions about people based on only a few facts?**

Say: **We need to make a real effort to get to know one another so we won't draw the wrong conclusions.**

Boldly Go...

OVERVIEW: Teenagers will learn more about each other as they discover what each values.

TIME INVOLVED: 10 to 15 minutes

SUPPLIES: index cards, pencils

PREPARATION: none

Pass out index cards and pencils. Tell teenagers that they've all been chosen to go on a very special mission to space. Unfortunately, there are severe luggage restrictions. Each person can take only one earthly thing along. Let the teenagers think a few minutes. As they're thinking, emphasize that they must leave absolutely everything behind except for what they write on their cards. Then have them write what they'll be taking on their cards and have them initial their cards. Collect the cards.

When you have all the cards, randomly call out three sets of initials at a time to group teenagers in trios. Return the cards.

Tell teenagers that their trios constitute mission teams. The members of each trio should share what they have written on their cards. Based on what their cards say, they should decide what their team mission should be. For example, if two mission team members say they would take their pets and the third member says he would take his car, the team's mission might be to go to a planet void of animals and start a traveling circus.

Give a few minutes for discussion, and then have one member of each team share their team's personal selections and their team mission.

Ask:

• **What did this activity tell us about what we care about or hold most important?**

• **What or who do you care most about or consider to be most important to you? Why?**

• **What one thing can we do to care more about each other?**

Say: **Each of us is important to God. And each of us can let one another know this in many different ways. The best way is by working hard to let others here know they are important to us.**

8

I've Got Your Number

OVERVIEW: Teenagers will get to know one another based on a set of numbered instructions.

TIME INVOLVED: 5 to 10 minutes

SUPPLIES: paper, pen, tape or straight pins

PREPARATION: Prepare a slip of paper with a number written on it for each person. Then prepare another slip of paper for each person with instructions written on it. (Make sure you have an instruction for each number.) The instructions might include the following: "Introduce four to three," "Shake hands with three and six," "Find out what two likes best for breakfast," and "Discover seven's birthday."

Give each teenager a slip of paper with a number on it, and have them tape or pin their numbers on their clothing where everyone can see them. Then have teenagers stand in a circle and give each person a slip of paper with an instruction written on it.

Explain that when you call out a number, the person with that number has to immediately carry out the instruction written on his or her slip of paper. As soon as the person finishes and returns to his or her place in the circle, call out another number. Keep the game going at a fast pace until you've called out all the numbers in the circle.

For extra fun, call out more than one number at a time. You may even want to prepare more than one instruction for each number and let kids keep playing!

Join the Circus!

OVERVIEW: Teenagers will work together to put on a circus.

TIME INVOLVED: 10 to 15 minutes

SUPPLIES: paper, pen

PREPARATION: Prepare several slips of paper, each bearing the name of a different circus group, such as clowns, bareback riders, trapeze artists, acrobats, or circus animals.

Have teenagers form groups of at least three. Give each group a slip of paper with the name of a circus group written on it. Tell them that the show must go on in three minutes! Groups have those three minutes to decide how to present their acts.

After three minutes, play Ringmaster and announce each group in turn. Let each group perform its part of the circus as the other groups applaud.

To add to the effect, provide a collection of props for groups to use in their acts. The props can include hats, kazoos, brooms, fake noses, or feather plumes.

Common Bonds

OVERVIEW: Teenagers will get into groups based on common bonds and have brief conversations.

TIME INVOLVED: 10 to 30 minutes

SUPPLIES: none

PREPARATION: none

Say: We're going to be getting to know each other a little better today. I am going to call out categories and divisions within each category. Then you will need to go to the category division that best fits you. Once you're all in your divisions, I'll read a question. Everyone in each division needs to take turns answering the question and discussing it with the others.

Call out a category and then tell teenagers where each division within the category should go. After teenagers form their divisions, ask the question. Then observe their conversations and call out a new category when it seems as though everyone has finished the discussion.

Following are some examples of categories, divisions, and questions. Feel free to add to the list.

Category 1—**Birth order:** oldest, middle child, youngest, only child
  • **Describe the member of your family you are most like.**

Category 2—**Length of residence in the area:** I've lived here my whole life, I've lived here about half my life, I've lived here less than a quarter of my life, I'm new here.

　　• **What's your favorite childhood memory?**

　• **Category 3—Free time:** hang out with friends, go to a concert or a movie, go shopping, watch TV

　　• **What's your favorite hobby or interest?**

　• **Category 4—Favorite class:** English or literature; math or science; drama, music, or art; PE; history, government, or economics; other

　　• **What career do you want to have?**

Greetings, Everyone!

OVERVIEW: Teenagers will get to know each other better as they form pairs by finding the missing halves of greeting cards.

TIME INVOLVED: 5 to 10 minutes

SUPPLIES: a variety of used greeting cards, scissors

PREPARATION: Cut off and throw away all but the front of each card. Cut each front by dividing the "headline" into two parts. For example, if a graduation card says "Congratulations" at the top, cut the card so that half says "Congrat" and the other half says "ulations."

Give each person half of a card. Make sure you distribute only halves of whole cards. If you have an odd number of teenagers, you should give one half card to yourself. Tell teenagers that they need to find the other half of their cards. Once teenagers have formed pairs by completing cards, have each pair create a singing telegram to deliver the card's message to the rest of the group.

Scrambled Cities

OVERVIEW: Teenagers will form groups and learn more about group members by discussing city names.

TIME INVOLVED: 5 to 10 minutes

SUPPLIES: name tags, a marker

PREPARATION: Choose several well-known cities in five or six different states, and scramble the letters in each city name. Write one scrambled city name on each name tag. Make sure you have one name tag for every person.

As teenagers arrive, give them each a name tag and tell them to unscramble their city names and then find the other people in the room whose cities are in that state. If teenagers don't know what states their cities are in, have them ask others. When teenagers have formed groups of cities by state, have them discuss the following questions:

• **Have you ever been to any of these cities? Tell about your experiences there.**

• **Which of these cities would you most like to visit? Why?**

Musical Circle Game

OVERVIEW: Teenagers will form circles and share information with each other.
TIME INVOLVED: 10 to 15 minutes
SUPPLIES: cassette player with a music tape
PREPARATION: none

Have teenagers form two circles of equal numbers, with one circle inside the other. Ask teenagers to walk around in the circle while the music is playing. When you stop the music, have teenagers turn and face the people opposite them and share their answers to each question you ask. If there's an odd number of teenagers, the one without a partner should share answers with you. When they've finished sharing, start the music again.

Here are some sample questions:
• **What's your favorite color?**
• **What's your favorite class in school?**
• **How many brothers and sisters do you have?**
• **What's your favorite Bible verse?**
• **What's your biggest pet peeve?**
• **If you could be any flavor of ice cream, what would you be and why?**

What Can You Hear?

OVERVIEW: Teenagers will listen carefully to outdoor sounds and discuss why listening is important in relationships.

TIME INVOLVED: 10 to 15 minutes

SUPPLIES: pens, paper

PREPARATION: none

Have teenagers form small groups of five or six, and give each group a pen and a sheet of paper. Tell the groups to go outside and listen carefully to everything they hear for five minutes. Then have them write a list of all the sounds they have heard. Ask the groups to come inside and share what they heard. Then have groups discuss the following questions:

• **Was this activity easy or difficult? Why?**

• **What things did you do to make it easier to hear the sounds around you?**

• **Why is listening important in your relationships?**

• **How can you become a better listener?**

Personal Dedications

OVERVIEW: Teenagers will learn special things about each other as they discover their favorite hymns or songs.

TIME INVOLVED: 20 to 30 minutes

SUPPLIES: pens, paper

PREPARATION: none

Give a piece of paper and a pen to each teenager, and have them pair up with another person. Tell teenagers to ask their partners what makes them special. Then have teenagers ask their partners what their favorite hymns or songs are and why. Finally, ask teenagers to write a song dedication for their partners in which they dedicate favorite songs because of special qualities. For example, someone might say, "I dedicate 'Awesome God' to John because he enjoys rafting, boating, and hiking, and he enjoys seeing God's awesome creation when he is doing those activities."

Have partners share their song dedications with the group.

E-Mail Encouragement

OVERVIEW: Teenagers will use e-mail to get to know each other better and to encourage each other.

TIME INVOLVED: 5 to 10 minutes

SUPPLIES: slips of paper, pens, a calendar, a bowl

PREPARATION: Prior to the meeting, ask each person to bring in his or her e-mail address (or the family's street address).

Distribute slips of paper and pens, and ask each person to think of a funny and clever e-mail address that describes a spiritual gift or biblical principle that each demonstrates in his or her life. For example, someone might think of Iprayforall@jesuslistens.god. Give teenagers five minutes to come up with their e-mail addresses. After the five minutes are up, ask teenagers to put the slips of paper in a bowl. Draw the slips out one at a time and have teenagers try to match each address with the correct person.

Then have teenagers copy down everyone else's real e-mail addresses. Be sure to include your own! If teenagers don't have home computers with e-mail access, pair them with group members who have e-mail. Once the address lists are complete, designate each teenager to send an "e-mail encouragement letter" to the rest of the group on a specific day of the week. Using the calendar, try to assign every day of the week, if possible. The letters can include Scripture verses, poems, funny jokes, stories, youth group updates, prayer requests, and words of appreciation for the rest of the group. The following week, bring in copies of all letters exchanged and discuss how special it was to receive (and anticipate) these e-mail encouragements.

Who Did It?

OVERVIEW: Teenagers will share anonymous off-the-wall activities and the rest of the group tries to guess "who did it."

TIME INVOLVED: 10 to 15 minutes

SUPPLIES: a bucket, index cards, pens, and a snack

PREPARATION: none

Give each person an index card and a pen. Tell the group to think of things they have done that others may not know about. Ask them to write their "unknown" activities on the cards, sign their names, and place the cards in the bucket.

Have the group get into a circle with guys on one side and girls on the other side. Explain that you will draw a card and read it out loud. If a guy has written the card, the girls will guess which guy wrote it. If a girl has written the card, the guys guess. You'll read the card and then say three guy's or girl's names. If the guessers are correct, they are awarded two points. If they're wrong, the guessees get a point.

After all of the cards have been read, have the group with the most points serve the other group a snack as they all talk about the new things they have learned about each other!

The Dot Game

OVERVIEW: Teenagers will try to take each other's colored dots by asking personal questions.

TIME INVOLVED: 5 to 10 minutes

SUPPLIES: paper, colored-dot stickers, scissors, hat

PREPARATION: Cut the colored-dot stickers into strips of five for each person.

Hand each person a sheet of paper and a strip of five colored-dot stickers. In this game, teenagers will get to know each other better while trying to collect colored-dot stickers. Here's how the game works. One person in the group asks each other person one question about himself or herself. If the person uses the catchword "because" when answering, the questioner can take one dot from that person. When players take dots, they should put them on their sheets of paper. If a player loses all of his or her original dots, he or she can play with the dots taken from other people. Players who lose all of their dots, are out of the game.

Variation: Put catchwords for each person on slips of paper that they can draw from a hat. This way each questioner is listening for a different word and the teenagers they are questioning are never sure what they shouldn't say!

Cowboy Creations

OVERVIEW: Small groups of teenagers will create cowboy and cowgirl characters.

TIME INVOLVED: 20 to 30 minutes

SUPPLIES: newspapers, tape, scissors, an instant-print camera (optional)

PREPARATION: none

Divide the teenagers into groups of four. Give each group a stack of newspapers, tape, and two pairs of scissors.

Announce to the entire group that they have twenty minutes to create a cowboy or cowgirl! Each group should choose a teammate to play the part. Then the others are in charge of making the western outfit.

After twenty minutes, call the cowboys and cowgirls to the front of the room. Have each group explain the different parts of the outfits they created. Take pictures of each group with their person in costume.

Next ask the cowboys and cowgirls to leave the room.

Have the remaining teenagers put several columns on a piece of paper, one for each cowboy and cowgirl. Have teenagers write each cowboy's or cowgirl's name at the top of a column. Explain that when you say "go," they need to write down as many details as possible about each cowboy or cowgirl costume. Give them three to five minutes to write down details. Then have the cowboys and cowgirls return to the room so everyone can see how good their memories were! If you take photos, hang them in the room to remind teenagers of the fun they had.

Toss 'n' Tell

OVERVIEW: Teenagers will each throw a ball in the air and tell as many things about themselves as possible before catching the ball.

TIME INVOLVED: 5 to 10 minutes

SUPPLIES: balls

PREPARATION: none

This game is best played outdoors. Have teenagers gather in a circle. If you have more than twelve students, have them form two circles. Ask students to think for a minute about what other people in the group might not know about them. For example, someone might "secretly" play the bassoon or love to watch professional soccer. Encourage everyone to think of as many bits of information as possible.

After students have thought a minute, give a ball to each group. Explain that each teenager will have a turn to throw the ball high into the air, say as many things as possible about himself or herself while the ball is in the air, and then catch the ball. Assure teenagers that the goal is not necessarily to catch the ball, but to tell—so that everyone can understand—as much about themselves as possible.

Have groups begin the game. After students have had a chance to tell about themselves, have groups play again—this time saying as many things about *other* people in the group as they can while the ball is in the air.

Hair, Mustache, Beard

OVERVIEW: Teenagers will race to find their matches and learn little-known facts about others in the group.

TIME INVOLVED: 10 to 15 minutes, longer for larger groups

SUPPLIES: paper, markers, and tape

PREPARATION: none

Tape a blank piece of paper to each person's back. Encourage teenagers to help one another do this while you give each person a marker.

Next show teenagers three gestures that will be used throughout the game: Hair—open hand on head with fingers extending onto forehead; Mustache—index finger resting below nose on upper lip; and Beard—cupped hand under chin.

Say: I will say, "Hair, mustache, beard," and on the word "beard," each of you should do one of the three gestures I have just demonstrated. You choose which gesture to make, but you must make one. With your hand still in place, race to find two others who complete the set. Each completed set should include three people—one hair, one mustache, and one beard. Have each person in your group sign his or her name on the paper on the other person's back and also write a little-known fact about himself or herself. You must give a different fact each time. Ready? Hair, mustache, beard!

Play as many rounds as time allows. Challenge teenagers to form new groups each time.

We Stick Together

OVERVIEW: Teenagers will create a tape ball to demonstrate that every word said impacts the whole group.

TIME INVOLVED: 10 to 20 minutes

SUPPLIES: masking tape

PREPARATION: Tear two strips of masking tape for each person.

Form a large circle. Give each teenager two strips of masking tape. Say: Tape one strip on top of the other. When you're finished, try to pull the strips apart.

Once teenagers have pulled their tape strips apart, ask:

• Now that you've stuck your tape once, it has less sticking power. Your tape may even be torn now. How is this like words we say and then try to take back?

• Every word we say sticks to both the person we say it to and the people who overhear it, like your two strips of masking tape. What kind of words will you choose as a result of this principle?

Call on teenagers one at a time to say something encouraging to someone else. Make sure no phrases are repeated. The first person forms a ball with his or her tape while speaking the encouragement. The next person adds his or her tape to the ball, and so on. When everyone has shared a phrase and added to the tape ball, ask:

• How is this tape ball like our group?

Puzzle Connections

OVERVIEW: Teenagers will link puzzle pieces as they form relationship connections through something they have in common.

TIME INVOLVED: 5 to 10 minutes

SUPPLIES: a jigsaw puzzle with around the same number of pieces as group members

PREPARATION: none

Give each person a puzzle piece, and challenge everyone to find another puzzle piece that fits it. When teenagers have formed pairs, have partners find one thing they have in common. Then have each pair find one other pair whose pieces link with theirs, and ask foursomes to find something they all have in common. Then have each foursome find another foursome and repeat the process. Have teenagers keep linking until the whole group can name one thing they all have in common.

The Power of Intentionality

OVERVIEW: Teenagers will arrange the letters in the word "intentionality."

TIME INVOLVED: 10 to 15 minutes

SUPPLIES: paper, marker, scissors

PREPARATION: Write each letter in the word "intentionality" on a separate sheet of paper, then cut the letters apart.

Give each person one letter. If your group has fewer than fourteen, give some teenagers more than one letter. Direct teenagers to arrange themselves to spell "intentionality." Ask:

• What is intentionality?

• What does an attitude of intentionality have to do with the relationships in our group?

Say: Connections happen best when we take the time to form them purposely. Now take some time to see how many words you can form with your letters.

19

As teenagers spell words, ask the members of each "word" group to name a way to intentionally form friendships with others in the group. Continue this process until teenagers have exhausted their word possibilities.

Say: **In the process of forming words, you also formed bonds with several different individuals.**

Ask:

• **What kinds of actions can you take to intentionally keep those bonds growing?**

Fantasy Tag

OVERVIEW: Teenagers will learn more about group members by guessing their fantasies.

TIME INVOLVED: 10 to 15 minutes

SUPPLIES: paper, pens

PREPARATION: none

Begin by giving each teenager a slip of paper and a pen. Explain that each teenager will need to write a fantasy on the slip of paper. This fantasy should be something the person has always wanted to do and won't mind having it read publicly. For example, someone's fantasy might be, "I've always wanted to go scuba diving off the coast of New Zealand."

Collect all the papers, then have students form teams of four. Explain that you'll be reading the fantasies aloud, one at a time. Teams will guess who each fantasy belongs to. If a team guesses correctly, the person whose fantasy was read becomes a member of the guessing team and the team gets another chance. The same team keeps guessing until they guess incorrectly.

Begin by reading all of the fantasies one by one. Then read them again, one at a time, and allow teams to guess. Play until all fantasies have been correctly identified. Then ask:

• **Did you learn anything new or unusual about any of the members of our group? If so, what?**

• **Why are our fantasies important parts of who we are?**

Bubble-Maker or Bubble-Buster?

OVERVIEW: Teenagers will interact with bubbles and learn how their words and actions can build people up or tear them down.

TIME INVOLVED: 5 to 10 minutes

SUPPLIES: bubble-making liquid with wand, lively Christian music and a CD player (optional)

PREPARATION: Consider enlisting the help of several others to help you blow bubbles so there are lots and lots of them.

Begin by simply blowing bubbles over group members' heads. If you brought some lively music, play it as you blow the bubbles and group members chase them. Notice that the first reaction of most teenagers will be to try to pop the bubbles. If anyone is trying to catch and hold the bubbles, take special note of that. Blow bubbles for about a minute. Then stop and instruct group members to try and catch bubbles in their hands without popping them. Ask:

• What was the reaction of most of us when the bubbles went flying all over the place? Why?

• Was it harder to pop bubbles or to catch them without popping them?

Say: The first reaction of most people was to pop the bubbles. After all, popping bubbles is much easier than catching them and holding them. The way people often treat one another is very similar. Too many of us are bubble-busters. We find it natural and easy to cut people down or to treat them unkindly—bursting their bubbles. Our words and actions can be devastating.

Building people up and loving them takes effort that doesn't always come naturally. Our words and actions can bring people joy if we will just make the effort. This is how our youth ministry can make a difference. Let's be bubble-makers, not bubble-busters.

Who? What? Where?

OVERVIEW: Teenagers will work together to guess pantomimes. This will emphasize the importance of clearly communicating with others in order to build relationships.

TIME INVOLVED: 20 to 30 minutes

SUPPLIES: "Who? What? Where?" handout (p. 23), scissors

PREPARATION: Photocopy the "Who? What? Where" handout and cut apart the assignments.

Have group members form five teams. Give each team one of the assignments from the "Who? What? Where?" handout. Tell team members that their job will be to involve the whole team in a sixty-second pantomime of their assignment. They should do this in such a way that the rest of the group will be able to guess **who** they are pantomiming, **what** the person is doing, and **where** he or she is doing it.

Allow teams to find private places where they can practice their pantomimes for five minutes away from the eyes of other group members. After five minutes, call the group back together and have teams perform their pantomimes one at a time. Encourage the rest of the group to guess what each team is pantomiming. If the group can't guess correctly, either allow the team more time to pantomime or tell group members what was being pantomimed.

After all teams have performed, lead the group in a big round of applause. Then ask:

• How did you feel as you tried to guess what each group was pantomiming? Why?

• What did you have to do in order to do well at this game? Explain.

• Just as poor or unclear communication could be a hindrance in playing this game well, how does poor or unclear communication hurt us in our relationships?

• How vital is clear communication in building close relationships with others? Explain.

• What are some things we can do in this group to communicate better and to get to know one another better?

Who? What? Where?

✂ --

ASSIGNMENT 1

Who? A yodeler

What? Fending off a mouse that is creeping up his leg

Where? On a New York subway

ASSIGNMENT 2

Who? A clown

What? Crossing a river filled with alligators

Where? At a zoo

ASSIGNMENT 3

Who? An elephant

What? Eating cotton candy

Where? At a gas station

ASSIGNMENT 4

Who? A church choir member

What? Carrying a water balloon

Where? On a bed of hot coals

ASSIGNMENT 5

Who? A small boy

What? Balancing a soft-drink bottle in his hand

Where? On a train track

Blindfolded Friend Find!

OVERVIEW: A blindfolded group member will find "friends" by tagging others to illustrate the importance of reaching out to others.

TIME INVOLVED: 10 to 15 minutes

SUPPLIES: blindfolds

PREPARATION: Clear furniture and other obstacles from the middle of the room.

Explain to students that they'll be tagged by a Friend Finder in this game. Select a group member to be the Friend Finder, blindfold the person, and have group members form a circle around him or her. Spin the Friend Finder around several times, and tell the Friend Finder to try to tag other group members. When the Friend Finder tags someone, that person is blindfolded and becomes another Friend Finder. The game is over when everyone is a Friend Finder. After the game, ask:

• How is this game like the way you make friends? How is it different?

• Would it be easier to befriend people if we didn't judge them by their appearances? Explain.

• As more and more people in the game became Friend Finders, how did finding friends become easier? Why?

• What can we learn from this game about the importance of reaching out to others in friendship?

• What are some practical things we can do to make our group a friendlier place to be?

• What can each of us do to become better friend finders?

Blink 181

OVERVIEW: Teenagers will share facts about themselves while blinking rapidly, to illustrate the importance of making the effort to get to know one another.

TIME INVOLVED: 5 to 10 minutes

SUPPLIES: slips of paper, pens or pencils
PREPARATION: none

Distribute slips of paper and pencils or pens to students. Tell students that in a moment, they'll need to hold their slips of paper at arm's length and write the five most important things others should know about them. For example, someone might write, "I am into all sports," "Sometimes I have really good ideas or opinions, but I don't share them," or "I am absolutely loyal to my friends." Tell teenagers that they must blink rapidly and constantly while they write. Give students about thirty seconds to write their facts.

Then have students quickly pair up. Have partners trade papers and read, at arm's length while blinking, what their partners have written about themselves. Ask:

teacher tip

If you have access to a strobe light, add to the effect of this game by turning the light on instead of having students blink.

• **How did you feel trying to write and read as you blinked?**

• **How was this like trying to get to know people without concentrating on seeing them as they really are? How is it like trying to get to know someone without spending time with him or her? How is it like trying to get to know someone based on only a few facts?**

• **What does it take to really get to know someone?**

• **Why is it important for us to know one another well in our group?**

• **What one thing can we do in our group to get to know one another better?**

Close by having students share with their partners or with the group their lists of five most important things to know about them.

The Early Years

OVERVIEW: Teenagers will try to identify one another's baby pictures and get to know each other better by sharing memories from their early years along with present insights about themselves.

TIME INVOLVED: 10 to 15 minutes

SUPPLIES: baby pictures of group members, a marker, poster board, glue or tape, paper, pens

PREPARATION: Ask students ahead of time to bring baby pictures of themselves taken before they turned two. Write "The Early Years" across the top of the poster board, and attach the baby pictures of group members to the poster board, identifying each one with only a number.

Distribute paper to group members, and have each person list down the left side of the paper the numbers you used on "The Early Years" board. Have group members now look closely at "The Early Years" board and guess who each picture is. Allow group members about two minutes to write names next to the numbers. When two minutes are up, identify the group member in each baby picture, allowing students to "grade" their papers to see how well they did. If you'd like, offer a candy prize to the person whose picture stumped the most people.

If you have a large group, have teenagers form small groups of four to six people for the following discussion. If your group is small, consider having group members sit in a circle and share their responses to each question. Ask:

• **What is your earliest childhood memory?**

• **What was your favorite toy when you were a child? favorite thing to do?**

• **What is your favorite thing to do now?**

• **What two words best described you as a child?**

• **What two words best describe you now? Explain.**

• **Was your childhood sad, happy, or just kind of average? Explain.**

• **In what way are you still the same as you were when you were a child? How are you most different?**

Mingle! Mingle! Mingle!

OVERVIEW: Teenagers will mingle and form hugging groups as they discuss reaching out to everyone in the group with friendship.

TIME INVOLVED: 5 to 10 minutes

SUPPLIES: none

PREPARATION: Clear all furniture and other obstacles from the center of the room.

Have all group members stand in the middle of the room. Explain that in a moment, you'll say: "Mingle! Mingle! Mingle!" and they're to mill around in the center of the room. When they hear you call out a number, teenagers will need to form hugging groups containing that number of people. Any group members who are left out and cannot find a group of the correct number are eliminated from the game.

Play several rounds of the game and then ask:

• **Those of you who were eliminated, how did it feel to be eliminated from this game so enthusiastically by others in the group?**

• **How is this like a youth group whose members don't extend friendship to others?**

• **What will happen to our group if we don't easily and deliberately extend friendship to new people and those without friends in the group? Explain.**

• **Would you describe our group as generally friendly or unfriendly? Why?**

• **What are some things we can do to become more friendly as a group?**

• **How can we offer opportunities to find friendships for new people and those without friends in the group?**

Say: **When we just hang around with our usual friends, we tend to eliminate others from our group who may be new or who may not have formed friendships with anyone in the group.**

Close with a big group hug.

Move Over, Van Gogh!

OVERVIEW: Teenagers will work together to create "masterpieces."

TIME INVOLVED: 10 to 15 minutes

SUPPLIES: paper, markers in four different colors

PREPARATION: none

Have teenagers form groups of four, and give each person a piece of paper and a different-colored marker. Have the members of each group sit with their backs to each other, and tell them that they cannot talk to each other for the remainder of this activity.

Explain that teenagers in each group will be working together to create four different masterpieces. Tell teenagers that when you tell them to start, they'll have thirty seconds to begin drawing a picture. It can be a picture of anything they'd like—even just an abstract picture. Tell them to start drawing, and after thirty seconds, have them stop and pass each paper to the person on the right. Instruct them to try to continue the drawings just as the original artists might have, and remind teenagers that they can't speak to each other. Give them another thirty seconds to continue the masterpieces.

Continue in this manner until each group member has contributed to all four drawings. Then have teenagers turn around and share their completed "masterpieces." Ask a few volunteers to share their pictures with the whole group. Ask:

• **Does your finished picture look like you originally envisioned it? If not, what's different about it?**

• **Did you find it easy or difficult to follow someone else's vision without any guidance? Explain.**

• **What does this activity tell us about the importance of communication?**

What Are You Doing?

OVERVIEW: Teenagers will work together to "pass" various activities around the circle.

TIME INVOLVED: 10 to 15 minutes

SUPPLIES: none

PREPARATION: none

Begin by asking teenagers to each think of an activity they could easily pantomime. For example, someone might choose "washing dishes" or "combing hair." Ask them not to share what they thought of yet. You'll need to think of a pantomime to begin this activity.

Have teenagers stand in a circle, and explain that they're going to pass their pantomimes around the circle. Tell them that you'll start by demonstrating your pantomime. The person on your right will ask you,

"What are you doing?" You'll reply by saying something completely different than the activity you're pantomiming—for example, if your action is washing the dishes, you might say, "I'm climbing a tree." Continue to do your pantomime while having this dialogue with the next person. The person who asked will then begin to pantomime the activity you said you were doing (in this case, climbing a tree). The next person in the circle will ask what that person is doing, then reply with the activity he or she thought of. Continue until the pantomimes have gone all the way around the circle.

Poker Face

OVERVIEW: Teenagers will work together to form poker hands, then get to know each other better.

TIME INVOLVED: 10 to 15 minutes

SUPPLIES: a deck of cards, newsprint or a dry-erase board and a marker

PREPARATION: Write these simple descriptions of winning poker hands on the dry-erase board or newsprint:

- Three of a kind—three cards of the same rank and two random cards
- Full house—three of a kind and two of a kind
- Flush—Any five cards of the same suit
- Straight—Five cards in numerical order of any suit
- Straight flush—Five cards in numerical order of the same suit
- Two pairs—two sets of cards of the same rank and one random card

questions

- If you could have dinner with anyone, living or dead, who would it be and why?
- Where would your ideal vacation be? Why?
- If you could be any animal, what would you be and why?
- Who is your favorite Bible character? Why?
- What's your silliest childhood memory?

This game works best with a very large group. Give each person one card. Explain that when you say "go," teenagers will form groups as quickly as they can by using their cards to form winning poker hands. Tell them they can use the list you've written for reference. Give teenagers a few minutes to familiarize themselves with the poker hands and ask any questions they may have.

Tell teenagers that when they think they've formed a winning hand, all members of the group should sit down. Then say: "Go!" You may need to help teenagers with determining poker hands during the first few rounds of this game. Have teenagers who can't form a hand form a group together.

When teenagers have all found groups, have them each answer a question you will read from the "Questions" box (in the margin on this page.) After everyone has answered a question, play another round. Encourage teenagers to form groups with new people. Continue in this manner until teenagers have been in several different groups and answered several different questions.

categories

- jobs
- rodents
- diseases
- kinds of rooms in your home
- sports that do not use a ball
- animals smaller than a dog
- old wives' tales
- things in a classroom
- animals bigger than a dog
- famous sayings
- fruits
- cars
- candy bars
- cereals
- insects

Gimme Five!

OVERVIEW: Teenagers will work together to name five items in a category.

TIME INVOLVED: 10 to 15 minutes

SUPPLIES: none

PREPARATION: none

Have teenagers form trios. Explain that the object of this game is for trios to try to name five items in a category that you will call out. When members of a trio can name five items, they need to jump up, begin high-fiving each other, and yell, "Gimme five!" Then trio members will share the items they came up with so that the rest of the group can verify them. When a trio has five verified items in the category, they've won the category! Have the rest of the group celebrate their victory with applause!

Use the "Categories" margin box, or create your own. Continue until teenagers tire of the game!

Identity Shopping

OVERVIEW: Teenagers will help one member of the group guess his or her new identity.

TIME INVOLVED: 10 to 15 minutes

SUPPLIES: none

PREPARATION: none

A sk one volunteer to leave the room for a few minutes. Explain to the rest of the group that they will choose the volunteer's new identity. For example, they may decide that he or she is a firefighter or a hippie. Tell the group to think of things the volunteer would need in order to "play the part." For example, a hippie might need a tie-dye shirt. When group members have decided on an identity and "equipment," ask the volunteer to return.

Ask the volunteer to guess the new identity the group has chosen for him or her. The volunteer will do this by asking group members, one at a time, what to buy in order to be properly outfitted in the new identity. Each group member can tell the volunteer only one item to buy, and the volunteer will have a chance to guess the identity after each item.

After the volunteer has guessed the identity, ask for another volunteer to leave the room. Continue until teenagers tire of the game.

Fave Rave!

OVERVIEW: Teenagers will get to know one another and build some common ground by comparing favorite things.

TIME INVOLVED: 10 to 15 minutes

SUPPLIES: none

PREPARATION: none

T o begin this activity, read a category from the following list. For example, if you say, "favorite song," teenagers should say aloud the title of their favorite song and form groups of two or three people who made the same choice. In these groups, each person should share why they chose this song and what they feel this tells others about them. Have students who choose things no one else chooses form a single group for discussion. Use as many or as few of these categories as you like:

- favorite song
- favorite position for watching television
- favorite band
- favorite free-time activity
- favorite toothpaste
- favorite school subject
- favorite thing to say
- favorite sport
- favorite writer or poet
- favorite movie
- favorite soap
- favorite food
- favorite words to hear from parents
- favorite television show
- favorite candy
- favorite color
- favorite ice-cream flavor
- favorite kind of pet
- favorite thing to do in the church youth ministry
- favorite soft drink
- favorite snack

(Just for fun, between favorite categories, consider playing loud music and letting group members "rave" for a few seconds.)

After the activity, lead a short discussion. Ask:

- **How did you feel sharing your favorites with others? Why?**
- **What was the most surprising thing you learned about others in this game? the most surprising thing you learned about yourself?**
- **What else did you learn?**
- **How can some of what we learned help our youth ministry?**
- **How might knowing more about what we share in common help us to form closer relationships?**

Trust
Builders

Building Blocks of Trust

OVERVIEW: Teenagers will learn about the "building blocks" of trust.

TIME INVOLVED: 15 to 20 minutes

SUPPLIES: cardboard or wooden building blocks, small squares of paper, pens, tape

PREPARATION: none

G ive one block, one square of paper, and a pen to each member of the group. (If your group is smaller than six, give each person two blocks and two paper squares.) Tell teenagers to think about the things that help them trust other people. Then ask each teenager to write one thing that helps build his or her trust in another person on his or her paper square. When they've finished writing, have them use tape to attach their paper squares to the sides of their building blocks. Then have teenagers build a tower using all of their blocks. Explain that they need to build the tower with just two blocks across and as high as it will go.

When the tower is built, have teenagers pull a piece out of the tower one at a time without making the tower fall. When a person pulls a piece out, ask him or her to read aloud what's written on the block and tell how he or she demonstrates that characteristic in life.

Continue in this manner until someone makes the tower fall. When this happens, have teenagers form pairs and discuss these questions:

• **Were all the things on the blocks important? Were there some that were more important than others? Explain.**

• **How is this experience like building trust?**

Who Can You Trust?

OVERVIEW: Teenagers will observe the skills and abilities of others and discuss who they would trust to help them in various situations.

TIME INVOLVED: 10 to 15 minutes

SUPPLIES: paper, pens

PREPARATION: Make a list of group members. Beside each name, note two things that person does well, enjoys doing, or knows a great deal about.

S ay: Let's talk a bit about trust. You may trust some people more than others when it comes to certain situations. For example, if you're having car trouble, you will probably be more likely to trust someone who has experience working on cars to help you. Let's discuss what situations you would trust the members of this group in.

Refer to your prepared list. Randomly select a skill or ability—such as good writing and composition skill. Ask a question such as, "If you were having trouble with an English term paper, who could you trust to help you troubleshoot?"

If the person's talent is known, someone in the group will probably suggest him or her.

If no one knows about the person's talent, or simply fails to come up with the person's name, you can recommend students and their skills.

Go through your entire list, suggesting situations in which each person's skills are called for at least twice. This process not only showcases everyone's abilities, but enables members to offer their best to others in the group.

Pass out paper and pens. Instruct everyone to write down the name of each person in the group. Beside each name, have teenagers write the one thing they know they can trust that person to do or be for them. When the lists are complete, encourage group members to keep their lists of "trusted friends" and refer to them when they need help.

A Penny for Your Thoughts

OVERVIEW: Partners will rely on each other to successfully toss and catch pennies.

TIME INVOLVED: 5 to 10 minutes

SUPPLIES: pennies, funnels (or paper rolled and taped into funnel shapes)

PREPARATION: none

Have teenagers form pairs and stand four feet apart facing each other. Give one partner in each pair ten pennies, and give the other partner a funnel.

The object of the game is to see how many pennies each pair can catch in its funnel. (If players seem to have trouble catching pennies at this distance, let partners move one or two steps closer. If catching is too easy, have them stand farther apart.) After one round of play, have partners switch roles.

After the game, discuss how partners had to trust each other's skills in order to be successful.

Bodyguard

OVERVIEW: Teenagers will act as "bodyguards" to protect each other.
TIME INVOLVED: 5 to 10 minutes
SUPPLIES: none
PREPARATION: none

Have teenagers form groups of three. Have each group choose one player to be the Star. The other two players will be the Bodyguards. Choose one group to go first, and have that group move to one end of your playing area. While one group is performing, the rest of the teenagers are the Fans, and they gather at the other end of the room.

Explain that the object of the game is for the Fans to tag the Star without being tagged by the Bodyguards. The Star and Bodyguards will try to travel from one end of the playing field to the other without the Star being tagged. The Bodyguards will join hands and travel in front of the Star as protection. If a Bodyguard tags a Fan, the Fan is out of the game and sits down. If a Fan tags the Star, they change places and play begins again.

After the game, discuss how no person can succeed totally alone and how we all need someone to protect us at times.

Blind Walk

OVERVIEW: Teenagers will practice trusting each other on a blind walk.

TIME INVOLVED: 20 minutes to 1 hour

SUPPLIES: blindfolds

PREPARATION: Find a safe trail or route that has a nice view at the end.

Say: Sometimes trusting God means following him when we don't know what's ahead. Today we are going on a little walk in the dark. Find a partner.

After everyone finds a partner, hand out blindfolds.

Say: **In your pair, one person will be blindfolded and the other person will lead him or her on the walk.**

Give teenagers time to put on the blindfolds. Then have pairs line up behind you.

Say: **Leaders, take care of your blindfolded partners. Follow me along the path. Oh, one more thing...you can't touch your partners. You can only give them verbal instructions.**

At the end of the walk, have teenagers take off the blindfolds and look at the view. Ask:

• **How did it feel to be blindfolded?**

• **How did it feel to be the leader?**

• **Leaders, was it difficult not to be able to touch your partners? Why?**

• **Have you ever had to trust God in this way?**

On the way back, have partners switch roles.

Team Trust

OVERVIEW: Teenagers will narrow down their definitions of trust.

TIME INVOLVED: 30 minutes to 1 hour

SUPPLIES: 100 index cards, pens, poster board, markers

PREPARATION: Prepare five to ten index cards with a wide range of opinions on the word "trust" (make sure you include negative ones). For example, write, "I don't trust people because I'm afraid they'll hurt me" and "I find it very easy to trust my friends to keep my secrets."

37

ive each teenager four blank index cards and a pen, and ask them each to write down four different opinions about the word trust on their cards. Tell them their opinions can be negative or positive and specific or general. After about five minutes, collect the cards and mix them with your pre-written cards. Randomly distribute three cards to each person. Ask teenagers to study the opinions on the cards, and then arrange them in order of personal agreement. Spread the leftover cards on a table with the opinion sides facing up.

Tell teenagers that now they can exchange any of the cards in their hands that they don't agree with for cards on the table. Allow an additional five minutes for this exchange. Now ask teenagers each to exchange at least one card with someone else. They can exchange more cards if they have time, but their goal is to get three cards with opinions closest to their own. Take a few minutes for this step.

Now tell the group to form teams of five. (If your group is smaller than twenty, form teams that will provide at least three final posters to discuss.) The goal for each team is to discard all of the team's cards except for three that they feel best describe the team's collective opinion about trust. Give teams five to ten minutes to discuss and discard.

Next give each team a piece of poster board and markers. Have teams each write their three opinions on their poster board. When teams are finished, have each team present its poster. Then ask the group:

• **How did you first think about your concept of trust?**

• **Did you find your teammates felt the same as you or differently? Explain.**

• **Why are there so many different opinions on what trust is and how one can be trustful?**

Box Game

OVERVIEW: Teenagers will see which team can move a group of empty boxes the fastest.

TIME INVOLVED: 15 to 20 minutes

SUPPLIES: several empty boxes of various sizes, masking tape

PREPARATION: Form a starting line and a finish line for each of two teams by putting masking tape on the floor. Make the lines three feet long, and space them twenty feet apart. Set several boxes near each team's starting line.

Have teenagers form two teams. Divide each team into halves, and have one half stand on the starting line and half on the finish line. Those standing on the starting line will designate one team member to be a human mover, ready to be loaded with boxes. After you say "go," members of each team will stack the boxes on the outstretched arms of the human mover. The human mover will run with the boxes balanced on his or her arms to the finish line and pass them to the next team member, who then becomes the human mover, and runs back to the starting line. Teams will continue in this manner until all team members have been human movers. If boxes fall off, the human mover who was carrying them must go back to the starting line and start again.

After the game is over, have teenagers sit in a circle. Then ask:

- **What was challenging about this game?**
- **Why was it important to trust your teammates?**
- **How did trust and teamwork factor into your success or failure?**

Bagel Pass

OVERVIEW: Teenagers will pass a bagel back and forth using pretzel sticks.

TIME INVOLVED: 10 to 15 minutes

SUPPLIES: six-inch pretzel sticks, bagels with large holes in the middle (more than you will need for the game in case someone drops a bagel while playing), cream cheese, plastic knives, some favorite beverages, cups

PREPARATION: none

Have teenagers form two groups. Then split each group in half, and have group halves stand about fifteen feet apart. Give each person a pretzel stick, and give each group a bagel. Have one group member at a time put a pretzel stick in his or her mouth and hold the bagel on the pretzel. Then have the group member walk to the other side and pass the bagel onto the next team member's pretzel. Continue in this manner until one group finishes. Dropped bagels call for starting over.

Let teenagers have their pretzels, bagels, and beverages as snacks. While they're eating, point out that one aspect of trust involves entrusting something important to someone else's care. Discuss how entrusting the bagel to another teammate helped teenagers work together as a team. Then discuss other ways this meaning of trust can be applied to teenagers' lives.

Blind Banana Splits

OVERVIEW: Help a blindfolded person build a banana split.

TIME INVOLVED: 10 to 15 minutes

SUPPLIES: bananas; ice cream; sundae toppings such as nuts, sprinkles, flavored syrups, whipped cream, and maraschino cherries; a sharp knife; blindfolds; bowls; spoons; and towels for cleanup

PREPARATION: Place ice cream, several bananas, and the sundae toppings in small bowls on each table where kids will be sitting.

Have teenagers form pairs. Tell them one partner is going to help a blindfolded partner build a banana split. Tell pairs that the only way they can help each other is by talking to each other.

Blindfold one partner in each pair. Direct the seeing partner to give instructions to the blindfolded partner to help him or her build a banana split. They should start by finding a banana and peeling it.

Note: To avoid injury, let the seeing partner slice the banana.

The blindfolded partner should tell the seeing partner what kind of toppings he or she wants on the banana split. It is then up to the seeing partner to direct the blindfolded partner to those toppings. When one banana split is finished, have the partners change places. Let them enjoy their creations when both have finished building.

Fort Night

OVERVIEW: Teenagers will get to know each other and build trust as they construct and "live in" homemade forts.

TIME INVOLVED: 30 minutes to 1 hour

SUPPLIES: old blankets or sheets; staplers; flashlights; duct tape; string or rope; art materials such as construction paper, scissors, and stickers; "backpacking" snacks such as trail mix, crackers, and bottled water or juice

PREPARATION: none

I t's best to use a room that already has a lot of chairs or pews. Divide teenagers into groups of five to eight. Have each group take blankets, a stapler, duct tape, and string or rope to create a fort. Provide art materials so that groups can decorate their forts as well. Give groups time to make their forts special.

Throughout this process, the teenagers can help themselves to the "backpacking" snacks.

Once they're well-fed and comfortable inside their forts, have each teenager share about two places in which he or she has stayed away from home. It might be a camp, a friend's house, or a tree house. However, one place should be true and the other should be untrue. The rest of the group members should guess which place is the lie and which is the truth. Each person should get a chance to share.

Afterward the forts make a cozy setting for small group Bible studies and sharing, or they can provide a setting for planning a future summer camping trip.

Protect Me!

OVERVIEW: "Bodyguards" will protect "workers" from paper wads.
TIME INVOLVED: 5 to 10 minutes
SUPPLIES: scrap paper
PREPARATION: none

U se this game at the beginning or end of a meeting, especially when you need to set things up or put things away. Have teenagers form three groups: the Workers, the Bodyguards, and the Throwers. Assign one Bodyguard to each Worker; the group of Throwers can have one person more or one less than the other groups.

Explain a task that you need the Workers to accomplish—setting up chairs for a meeting or putting away supplies after a meeting, for example. Then explain that the Throwers will be wadding up scraps of paper and tossing them at the Workers and that the Bodyguards will be trying to bat away the paper wads so the Workers can work. Encourage the Workers to trust their Bodyguards instead of paying attention to the Throwers and the paper wads.

When everyone understands how to play, have Throwers begin making and throwing paper wads, and have the Workers begin working. After about a minute, stop the play. Have groups switch roles; Throwers can gather the used paper wads instead of making new ones. Have groups play again for a minute, then switch roles again.

After everyone has played each role, ask teenagers to assume the role of the Workers, complete the work, and gather the paper balls to put back into the recycling bin.

Popcorn Peril

OVERVIEW: Partners will lead each other through a field of popcorn.

TIME INVOLVED: 10 to 15 minutes

SUPPLIES: plain popped popcorn, blindfolds

PREPARATION: Spread the popcorn outside on a hard surface; teenagers will maneuver through the popcorn for about fifty feet. Spread enough popcorn so that it will be difficult—but not impossible—to maneuver without stepping on popcorn.

Take teenagers outside, and have them gather at one end of the area sprinkled with popcorn. Depending on the size of your group, have students form pairs or groups of up to six, and distribute blindfolds to each group.

Explain that the goal is for everyone to walk blindfolded through the field of popcorn without stepping on it. Tell teenagers that each blindfolded person will have a partner who can use only his or her voice to guide them.

Have one person in each group put on the blindfold, and emphasize that teenagers will need to trust each other to get through the field of popcorn. Say: **The partners should use only their voices to direct the blindfolded people's steps. When the blindfolded person gets to** the other side of the popcorn field, switch roles to return. If the teenagers are in groups, have them play the game as if it's a relay race.

When everyone understands how to play, begin the game. If someone steps on the popcorn, allow the play to continue since the goal is for one partner to help the other.

Have youth gather the popcorn after the game and use it to feed birds.

Conversation Cube

OVERVIEW: Teenagers will form teams, toss a giant cube, and do what it says.
TIME INVOLVED: 10 to 15 minutes
SUPPLIES: a square cardboard box, tape, newsprint, a black marker
PREPARATION: Tape the flaps of the box shut. Cover the sides of the box
  with newsprint and write one of the following phrases on each side: A Song,
  A Story, A Secret, A Sound Effect, A Statue, and Skip.

Divide the group into teams of three or more people. Say: **Each team will take turns rolling the cube and doing what it says—posing as statues, singing a song, sharing a story or a secret, or making a sound effect. If your team rolls Skip, pass the cube to the next team.**

Continue rolling the cube as time allows. Afterward, ask:

• **Did you feel relieved when your team rolled a Skip?**

• **Did you feel uncomfortable telling any secret or story to the rest of the group?**

• **Are there secrets or stories you felt you couldn't really share?**

• **What things can we do as a group to develop an environment of openness? How can we learn to trust one another with our friendship?**

• **How can we make visitors and newcomers feel at ease?**

Radioactive River Crossing

OVERVIEW: Teenagers will work together to complete a task.
TIME INVOLVED: 20 to 30 minutes

43

SUPPLIES: six large circles of cardboard or wood; two three-foot pieces of string or yarn; balls, hoops, and other items

PREPARATION: Create the banks of the river by laying the pieces of string about twenty feet apart.

Point to the "river" and say: **The waters of this river are filled with radioactive waste and they're very dangerous. It's your job to get everyone across the river without falling into it. To help you, these "turtles"** (point to the cardboard or wood circles) **will allow you to stand on their backs. However, if there isn't at least one foot on a turtle at all times, the turtle will get bored and swim away. If a person touches the radioactive waste, he or she will be given a handicap** (point to the balls, hoops, and other items) **to carry across the stream.**

Make sure everyone understands the rules. Place the turtles in the river strategically to make the crossing possible but difficult. As teenagers are crossing the stream, watch to make sure that all the turtles are being touched. If one isn't being touched, rush in and take it away, saying: **Oops! That turtle got bored!** Watch also for teenagers who accidentally touch the radioactive waste and hand them balls, hoops, or other items to hold as they cross.

After teenagers have crossed the stream, discuss these questions:

• **Was this experience easy or difficult? Explain.**
• **In what ways did you have to trust each other?**

Blind Bump

OVERVIEW: Teenagers will move blindfolded through a room while others guide them by instructions.

TIME INVOLVED: 5 to 10 minutes

SUPPLIES: a blindfold

PREPARATION: none

Ask one person to be "It" and blindfold this person. Ask everyone else to scatter across the room and stand, sit, or squat. Tell teenagers that once they're in place, they can't move from their locations or positions. The goal is for "It" to walk safely back and forth across the room, bumping as few people as possible. Select two people to be Guiders to help lead "It" back and forth across the room. One Guider will give clear and precise directions, and the other Guider will give directions that will make "It" bump into teenagers all along the way. "It" has to decide which Guider is telling him or her the truth. Once "It" has returned to the start, remove the blindfold and repeat the game with a new "It" and two new Guiders. Have the other teenagers change positions. Continue until everyone has had the chance to be "It." Then ask:

• **Was this game frustrating? Why or why not?**

• **Was it easy or difficult to tell who was giving true directions? Explain.**

• **Once you determined who was telling the truth, would you say your trust in this person increased or diminished? Why?**

• **What can this game teach you about placing your trust in the wrong people?**

• **What are some things we can do to distinguish voices leading us in the right direction from those trying to trip us up?**

Trust Enablers

OVERVIEW: Teenagers will gain an awareness of disabilities as they learn to trust each other more.

TIME INVOLVED: 15 to 20 minutes

SUPPLIES: "Trust Enablers" handout (p. 47); scissors; blindfolds; old sheets cut into long strips; wooden blocks; wax paper; hole punch; yarn or twine; cotton balls; snack food that needs to be assembled, such as sandwiches or ice cream sundaes

PREPARATION: Cut apart the sections of the "Trust Enablers" handout. You'll need one section for each pair of teenagers. Set out all of the non-snack supplies where they'll be easily accessible. Set out the snack supplies in another area of the room or in another room.

Have teenagers form pairs, and give each pair a handout section. Say: **We're going to do an exercise in trust that also shows you what it could be like to be disabled. One partner in your pair will be** disabled. The other partner will be the helper. You choose which is which. Read the instructions on your handout section and then use the supplies to create your disabilities.

Give teenagers a few minutes to do this and then say: **Now it's time to make snacks! Helpers, you'll need to help your disabled partners get to the area where the snacks are. Then you'll need to help make their snacks.**

While teenagers are eating their snacks, ask:

• **Those who were disabled, what was it like to trust your partner?**

• **Those who were helpers, what was it like to help another person?**

Shoe Sort

OVERVIEW: Teenagers will arrange themselves in order by shoe size as they gain trust in each other.

TIME INVOLVED: 10 to 15 minutes

SUPPLIES: none

PREPARATION: none

Have teenagers stand in a line, shoulder to shoulder, and close their eyes. Then explain that they've all become mute. Their job is to rearrange themselves by shoe size, from smallest to largest, without opening their eyes or talking.

You may need to spot while teenagers do this to help avoid bumped heads.

After teenagers think they've lined up correctly, have them open their eyes and check the results. Ask:

• **Did you find this activity frustrating? Why or why not?**

• **Why is communication such an important part of trust?**

Instant Impulse

OVERVIEW: Team members will trust each other to send the correct impulse.

TIME INVOLVED: 10 to 15 minutes

Trust Enablers

✂ ---

You are blind. Have your helper put a blindfold on you.

You are deaf. Put cotton balls in your ears. (You'll probably still be able to hear, so be sure to act as though you can't.)

You have the use of only one arm or leg. Have your helper immobilize an arm or leg with strips of a sheet.

You are visually impaired. Have your helper punch holes on either side of a wax paper square so your ears can hear, and then tie the wax paper around your head so it covers your eyes.

You have difficulty walking. Have your helper tie a wooden block to the bottom of one of your shoes.

You can't speak. You need to find another way to communicate with your helper.

You are mentally disabled. Act confused, and do the opposite of what your helper asks you to do.

SUPPLIES: a quarter, a small foam ball
PREPARATION: none

Have teenagers form two equal-sized teams. Have members of each team stand side by side and hold hands. The two teams should stand about one foot apart, facing each other. Appoint a leader for each team. These leaders should be across from each other at the same end of the line. Place the foam ball at the other end of the line from the leaders, equidistant from both teams. Stand near the leaders, and ask all team members except the leaders to close their eyes. The team members closest to the ball will put their free hands on their knees.

Explain that you'll flip a coin and the leaders of the teams will watch to see which end is up. If it's heads, each team leader will pass an "impulse" down the line by squeezing the hand of the person next to him or her. That person will squeeze the next person's hand, and so on. When the impulse reaches the last person, he or she will try to grab the ball. The team who grabs the ball first wins the round. When a team wins a round, its players rotate so the grabber moves to the front of the line and becomes the leader. If a coin lands on tails, nothing happens. However, if an overeager leader sends an impulse when the coin lands on tails, that team is assessed the penalty of having to "reverse rotate" its members one position. Play continues until the person who began as the leader becomes the leader a second time.

When the game is finished, ask:
• How was trust an important part of this game?
• Why is it important to trust people you're working with?

Trust Wave

OVERVIEW: Teenagers will trust each other as they run through a gantlet of group members, who will raise and lower their arms at just the right time.
TIME INVOLVED: 15 to 20 minutes
SUPPLIES: masking tape
PREPARATION: You'll need a large space for this game.

ave teenagers form two equal-sized groups, and have groups line up facing each other. Groups are the correct distance apart when players hold their arms straight out from their shoulders and the hands of the players on one side touch the wrists of the players on the opposite side.

When teenagers have lined up, place a masking tape line on the floor about twenty-five feet away. Teenagers in the gantlet will need to hold their arms out in front of them. Explain that a runner will start at the masking tape line and run, walk, or jog at a consistent speed through the aisle. Each player will need to raise his or her arms just in time for the runner to go through and lower his or her arms as soon as the runner has passed. When this is done correctly, it produces a wave effect.

Tell teenagers that you'll be the first runner. You may want to walk through the first time so teenagers can try this out more slowly. After you've gone through the aisle, ask for a volunteer to go next, and take his or her place in line.

Continue in this manner until everyone who wants to try going through the gantlet has had a chance. Then ask:

• **Runners, what was it like to go through the gantlet? How did you feel before? After?**

• **Players on the gantlet, did you find it easy or difficult to raise and lower your arms at the right times? Explain.**

• **How did this activity require trust? Did you feel that you could trust the other group members? Why or why not?**

Rain, Rain, Go Away

OVERVIEW: Teenagers will work together to make "rain."
TIME INVOLVED: 5 to 10 minutes
SUPPLIES: none
PREPARATION: A quiet spot is best for this game.

ave teenagers form a standing circle, and then have each person turn to face his or her left. Have teenagers get close enough to each other so they can easily touch the back of the person in front of them. Join in the circle with the teenagers.

Explain to the group that they're going to work together to make "rain." Encourage them to listen carefully during this activity. You may want to have them close their eyes. Explain that you will start a motion on the back of the person in front of you. When that person feels the motion, he or she will "pass" it on to the person in front of him or her. This will continue until the motion has gone all the way around the circle. Then you can start the next motion.

Here is the motion sequence:

• With your palms flat on the back of the person in front of you, make a rotating movement to achieve a swishing sound. This represents the sound of the wind before a rain shower.

• Gently and slowly tap your fingertips on the back of the person in front of you. This represents the first raindrops.

• Tap your fingertips a little harder and faster on the back of the person in front of you. This represents harder rain.

• Quickly "slap" your open palms on the back of the person in front of you. (Don't do this too hard!) This represents very hard rain or hail.

• Tap your fingertips a little harder and faster on the back of the person in front of you. This represents harder rain.

• Gently and slowly tap your fingertips on the back of the person in front of you. This represents the last raindrops.

• With your palms flat on the back of the person in front of you, make a rotating movement to achieve a swishing sound. This represents the sound of the breeze after a rain shower.

• Stop and wait for all sounds to cease.

After the "rain shower" is over, ask:

• **What did you think of this experience?**

• **Why do you think trust was necessary in this experience?**

Unity Builders

Identity Crisis

OVERVIEW: Teenagers will become more observant and aware of other group members.

TIME INVOLVED: 10 to 15 minutes

SUPPLIES: paper, pens

PREPARATION: As teenagers gather and chat before the meeting begins, take mental note of their appearance. Note things such as clothing color and style, hairstyle, and perfume or cologne. Also, listen in on conversations to discover facts about group members' lives. You may want to write things down if you can do so discreetly. Try to discover two facts for each group member, and make a numbered list of all the facts.

Have everyone sit in a circle on the floor. Distribute paper and pens to everyone and tell them to write the numbers that you have on your list.

Say: **Now it's time for a pop quiz! Are you all ready? I need you all to turn around so that you can't see anyone else. You can't look around the room or at anyone else during the quiz.**

Go down your list in order, and turn each fact into a question for group members to answer. For example, you can ask things like, "Who in this group is wearing a Hawaiian print shirt?" or "Who is wearing Calvin Klein cologne?" When you're finished with the quiz, have teenagers turn around and face the center of the circle. Begin with the top of your list and ask the questions again, allowing group members to express their answers—and, if need be, correct them. Have group members total their correct answers. Ask:

• **How observant do you feel you are? Explain.**

• **Why is it important to listen to others and notice things about them?**

Repeating this game periodically can motivate teenagers to pay greater attention to others in the group.

Braids

OVERVIEW: Teenagers will work together to make a giant braid.

TIME INVOLVED: 10 to 15 minutes

SUPPLIES: several different colors of yarn, scissors

PREPARATION: Cut enough ten-foot lengths of yarn for each team of four to six teenagers to have three lengths, each a different color.

Divide your group into teams of four to six, and give each team three pieces of yarn. Have the members of each team work together to produce a braid.

When teams are finished with their braids, say: **I'd like you to take a moment to look at your braid. Notice the different colors and how they're woven together.** Ask:

• **How does your braid remind you of working together with others?**

The completed braids may be cut into pieces to make friendship bracelets or necklaces that your group members may wear or offer to each other as a sign of unity and support.

Hand in Hand

OVERVIEW: Teenagers will connect to one another as they create a giant chalk mural on cement or asphalt.

TIME INVOLVED: 10 to 15 minutes

SUPPLIES: sidewalk chalk

PREPARATION: none

You'll need a large, clean concrete or asphalt area for this game—a vacant parking lot would do nicely. Divide the group into two large teams. Each team will make chalk outlines of group members on the ground, with each person's outline touching at least one other person's outline.

Say: **In this game, you'll need to help each other make chalk outlines. Take turns lying on the ground on your backs. Another person on your team will trace your outline in chalk. Be sure that** your outline is touching someone else's outline, so that all of our outlines will be connected when they're finished.

If you'd like, have the teenagers write their names inside their outlines. This game leads well into a discussion about unity and what it means to be connected to others.

Bucket Brigade

OVERVIEW: Teenagers will work together to fill a large receptacle with water.

TIME INVOLVED: 10 to 15 minutes

SUPPLIES: four large washtubs or small plastic pools (the kind used for small children), one bucket for each person

PREPARATION: Fill two washtubs or pools with water.

This is a perfect outdoor game for a hot day! Begin by dividing your group into two teams. Fill two washtubs or pools with water, assigning one to each team. Give each team an empty washtub or pool, an equal number of buckets, and have them stand in line between their pool full of water and their empty pool.

Say: **The object of this game is to fill your pool. The way you'll do this is by forming a human line from your full pool to your empty pool. One person fills a bucket and then empties the contents of the bucket into the next person's bucket. Continue in this manner until the water reaches the last person, who dumps it into the pool.**

When the pools are full, ask:

• **How did you have to work together to complete your task?**

• **Was this easy or difficult? Explain.**

• **How was filling the pool together like other things we need to accomplish as a group?**

When the game is over, use the water to water a garden, wash a car, or do some cleaning.

Picture Perfect

OVERVIEW: Teenagers will work together to create captions for old photographs.

TIME INVOLVED: 30 to 40 minutes

SUPPLIES: a stack of old photographs, paper, pens

PREPARATION: Number the photographs consecutively by writing a small number on the back of each one.

Have teenagers form two groups, and give each group a sheet of paper and a pen. Have each group number its sheet of paper according to the number of photographs you have. Say: **We're going to work together to create funny captions for some old photographs. Here's how this will work: I'll hold up a photograph, and each group will create its own caption for the photograph. Write your caption on your paper next to the number assigned to the photograph. We'll share them all in a few minutes.**

Begin by showing a few photographs and sharing a few examples of your own funny captions. Then show a photograph and give groups a minute or so to create their own funny captions. Continue in this manner until you've shown all the photographs.

Then show the photographs again in order, pausing after each one to allow groups to share their captions with the whole group.

Trash Collectors

OVERVIEW: Teenagers will work together in teams on a trash scavenger hunt.

TIME INVOLVED: 10 to 20 minutes

SUPPLIES: a plastic trash bag for each team; chocolate pudding, whipped topping, crushed chocolate sandwich cookies, bowls, spoons (optional)

PREPARATION: none

Divide the group into teams of three to five. Give each team a trash bag, and say: **This game will help us work together to make our world a cleaner place. Each team will have twenty minutes to fill its bag with trash.**

Be sure to set a safe boundary for this game—you may consider playing the game in a public park or other public area. Also, be sure to have a way to properly dispose of the trash after it's collected, and try to recycle as much trash as possible.

When the teams have returned, dispose of the trash—or set it aside for later disposal. Then ask:

• **What did you learn about our environment from this game?**

• **What do you think our role might be in caring for God's creation?**

• **How can we work together to fulfill our role in caring for God's creation?**

If you'd like, celebrate the cleanup by serving "mud pie" (chocolate pudding mixed with crushed chocolate sandwich cookies and whipped cream).

State Plates

OVERVIEW: Teenagers will discover each other's good qualities as they create license plates that represent group members.

TIME INVOLVED: 5 to 10 minutes

SUPPLIES: paper, crayons, colored markers

PREPARATION: none

Have teenagers form groups of three or four. Give each group a sheet of paper and a supply of colored markers and crayons.

Explain that each small group will create a state license plate that represents the personalities of its members. Each person in the group must contribute to the picture on the license plate, and the group must come up with a slogan for its state. Groups can use already-existing states, or they can create fictional states.

This game can take many directions. For example, groups can focus on dreams and aspirations, accomplishments, favorite sports or foods, or even combinations of letters and numbers significant to group members. The goal is for each group to create a unified license plate that encompasses aspects of and input from each member of the group.

When groups are ready, let them present and explain their license plates to the rest of the group.

Too Close for Comfort

OVERVIEW: Teenagers will "squish" together to fit themselves into a small area that continues to get smaller.

TIME INVOLVED: 15 to 20 minutes

SUPPLIES: masking tape

PREPARATION: none

Say: To set this game up, you'll all need to stand in the middle of the room in a tight group.

Once teenagers have formed a tight group, put masking tape on the floor around them. Then have everybody step out of the taped circle, and lay down another tape one-quarter of the way into the first circle.

Say: **Now comes your challenge—you'll all need to work together to squish everyone inside the new circle without any part of anyone's body touching the tape on the ground.** (If bodies lean outside of the taped area, that's OK.)

When teenagers accomplish this goal, move the tape in farther and have the group try to squish into smaller and smaller circles. Afterward, debrief the group by asking these questions:

• **Did you feel uncomfortable in such tight quarters? Why or why not?**

• **Did you feel like your voice was heard in developing a strategy? Why or why not?**

• **Who took charge of the group? Why?**

• **Do you feel that you were successful as a group? Explain.**

That Which We See

OVERVIEW: Teenagers will discover that they can accomplish greater things as a team than they can as individuals.

TIME INVOLVED: 20 minutes

SUPPLIES: paper, pens, a penny for each person (It's best to find several pennies from the same years—six from 1997, six from 1968, and six from 1981. That way, you can group teenagers by penny year.)

PREPARATION: Prepare a handout for each youth with the following headings and room to write between each one: I. What I See on the Front; 2. What I See on the Back; 3. General Characteristics.

Give each teenager the handout you prepared, a pen, and a penny. Then have them spend about five minutes studying their pennies and writing down what they see in the three categories on their handouts. At the end of the five minutes, tell teenagers to find the other people in the room with the same dates on their pennies.

Give each penny group a new sheet of paper, and have group members combine their lists into a collective list. Challenge them to work together to come up with more characteristics than those they saw before. Give groups five more minutes for this task.

When the time is up, have the groups come back together and share their findings. Then ask:

• **Did you see more in your pennies as individuals or as a group? Explain.**

    • **Why is it often easier for groups to come up with solutions?**

    • **What are some decisions that are best for a group to make?**

    • **What issues do we need to discuss as a group?**

    • **What decisions do we need to make as a group?**

Trust Shopping

OVERVIEW: Teenagers will work together to purchase all of the items on a shopping list.

TIME INVOLVED: I hour

SUPPLIES: blindfolds

PREPARATION: This game works best at a shopping mall or a large store. Prepare a list of items in advance that each group of teenagers can purchase for under twenty dollars. Some item ideas might be: a can of pop—the flavor choice is made by the shopper; a small bottle of perfume—the shopper will choose the brand based on scent; and a small stuffed animal—team members can describe various stuffed animals to shoppers to help them make a decision. Have each person bring five dollars to the meeting to cover the cost of this event.

Divide teenagers into teams of four. Have each team blindfold one member. Say: **Today you're going to go on a special shopping spree! You'll be working in teams to purchase a list of items. Your blindfolded member will be your team's shopper. The other team members may help the shopper, but the shopper has the final say about the items to be purchased.** Give each team a list of four items to purchase and twenty dollars, and give groups one hour to complete this task. Meet at a designated location and debrief the experience using the following questions.

Ask the blind shoppers:

• **How did it feel to be blind?**

• **Were there certain descriptions that were more helpful than others?**

• **What kinds of things did you need to trust the group?**

Ask other group members:

• **How did you feel about shopping with a blind person?**

• **What role did you need to play in order to help your shopper?**

Ask everyone:

• **What did this experience teach you about working together and helping each other?**

Donate all the items you purchased to a local shelter.

Hoop Race

OVERVIEW: Teenagers will form relay teams and race while rolling Hula Hoops.

TIME INVOLVED: 20 to 30 minutes

SUPPLIES: Hula Hoops

PREPARATION: Mark out a relay course around a large room or on an outdoor field.

Have teenagers form teams of four. Point out where the relay course is, and give each team a Hula Hoop. Tell teams that their goal is to roll their Hula Hoops from one end of the course to the other. Each member of the team needs to take a turn rolling the Hula Hoop. It's up to team members to decide the best way to accomplish this task.

If, at any time during the race, a team's Hula Hoop falls, the team must start over at the beginning.

Encourage teams to begin by creating strategies. Then cheer them on as they race. After the race is over, talk about how important it was for each relay team to work together to create a good strategy and accomplish its goal.

Bookmark Praying

OVERVIEW: Teenagers will create bookmarks with group members' prayer requests on them and commit to praying for these requests during the coming week.

TIME INVOLVED: 20 to 30 minutes

SUPPLIES: Bibles, concordances, poster board, rulers, scissors, markers, assorted glitter and small stickers for decoration

PREPARATION: Cut the poster board into 8x3-inch strips. You'll need one strip for each person.

Have teenagers form groups of four, and give each group a Bible and a concordance. Give each person a strip of poster board, and set out the other materials where they'll be easily accessible. Tell students that they're going to discover more about praying for each other. First, have each group look up a verse or passage about prayer. Have them use their concordances and Bibles to find a good verse or passage. Then tell groups that you'd like them to teach the rest of the group the verses or passages they chose. They can do this by creating a short skit or pantomime to demonstrate the actions that God asks of us. Give groups several minutes to create their skits or pantomimes. Then have each group present its verse or passage to the whole group. Ask:

• **What do these passages tell us about the importance of praying for each other?**

• **How could praying for each other make us closer as a group?**

Say: **Now I'd like you to work within your groups to create prayer bookmarks. First, I'd like you to write your favorite passage or verse about prayer on the top of your bookmark. Then have everyone in your group tell one prayer request he or she would like the group to** pray about during the coming week. Write each prayer request on your bookmark. If you have time, think of some things you'd like to pray about as a group, such as praying for victims of natural disasters or praying that God will work in the hearts of people at your school who don't know him. You can take your bookmarks home to remind you to pray every day for the people in your group.

Give groups ten minutes to complete their bookmarks. The next week, ask teenagers how they felt about praying for each other.

Connect-o-Blast!

OVERVIEW: Teenagers will form human "amoebas" by connecting their body parts.

TIME INVOLVED: 5 to 10 minutes

SUPPLIES: a Bible, newsprint, a marker, masking tape, a pair of dice

PREPARATION: Write the following on a sheet of newsprint: 2—head, 3—right elbow, 4—left elbow, 5—right knee, 6—left knee, 7—right hip, 8—left hip, 9—right foot, 10—left foot, 11—right hand, 12—left hand. Tape the newsprint to a wall.

Gather the group in front of the newsprint. Have the person whose birthday is closest to January 1 step forward. This player will start the game. Explain that he or she is going to roll the dice on the floor. Whatever total number is shown on the two dice will match a body part listed on the newsprint. When the player sees the number and finds the matching body part on the list, he or she must choose another person in the group and connect the designated body part with the same body part of the other person. For example, if the first player rolls a combined total of seven, that person connects his or her right hip to the right hip of another group member. Once two players have been connected, the dice are handed to another person who rolls and continues the game. This time, all three players connect body parts. Continue until everyone has rolled the dice and group members are all connected to each other.

Then read 1 Corinthians 12:12-20 aloud, and ask:

• **What was challenging about this activity?**

• What can this activity teach us about belonging to a group?

• Why do you think God wants us to care about one another? to consider one another to be very important? Explain.

If your group is close enough, point to each group member in turn and have all other group members say what the group would miss out on if that person was not part of the group.

Chain Game

OVERVIEW: Teenagers will work together to create a paper chain.

TIME INVOLVED: 5 to 10 minutes

SUPPLIES: construction paper, several rolls of tape or staplers

PREPARATION: Cut construction paper into 1x6-inch strips. There should be a generous supply for each team. Set up four stations. Each station needs a supply of the paper strips and tape or a stapler.

Divide the group into four teams. Direct each team to a different station. Say: **We're going to see which team's paper chain is the longest when the game is over. When I say "go," team members will form circles with the strips of paper and link the circles together to form chains. Make as long a chain as you can in sixty seconds. Ready? Go!**

After sixty seconds, have each team leave the chain it started and rotate to another station. Again, give teams sixty seconds to lengthen the chains as much as they can. The game is over when all teams have rotated to all four stations.

Have a representative from each team count the number of links at the team's last station. All four chains should be a similar length since all four teams helped to create each chain. Point out that working together on the chains has made all the teams winners. Link the four chains together, and hang the finished paper chain in the room to remind teenagers that working together accomplishes many things.

Building a Church

OVERVIEW: Teenagers will plan and construct a paper church.

TIME INVOLVED: 10 minutes

SUPPLIES: paper, rolls of tape, pens

PREPARATION: none

Have teenagers form teams of three or four. Give each team a supply of paper, a roll of tape, and a pen. Tell teams that they each have five minutes to plan a way to construct a church building with the paper and the tape. They can draw plans or just talk about the construction, but they can't begin building yet. Remind teams that a completed church building has a steeple.

When the five minutes is up, tell teams that they now have five minutes to build their churches. However, they must do their building in complete silence.

When the next five minutes is up, have each team show its completed church. Ask:

- **What was it like to build your church without talking?**
- **Was it easy or difficult to work together? Explain.**
- **How did you communicate with each other since you couldn't talk? How well did this work?**
- **What does this tell you about the importance of good communication?**

House of Cards

OVERVIEW: Teenagers will attempt to build a house of cards despite distraction.

TIME INVOLVED: 5 to 10 minutes

SUPPLIES: a deck of cards

PREPARATION: none

Have teenagers form two groups, A and B. Have members of Group A form a circle and place a deck of cards inside the circle. Members of Group B will stand outside the circle.

Explain that members of Group A will attempt to build a house of cards, while members of Group B try to thwart them. Group B may try to distract Group A by making noise or by crawling around the circle and trying to blow down the house of cards.

Call time after a few minutes, and discuss how unity is destroyed in a group or a relationship when people work against one another instead of working in harmony.

Gotcha!

OVERVIEW: Teenagers will help each other keep from crossing their arms or legs during a meeting.

TIME INVOLVED: length of meeting

SUPPLIES: bows or ribbons

PREPARATION: none

A t the beginning of a meeting, explain that teenagers will be play-ing a game throughout the meeting. Say: **I'm setting a new rule for our meeting today. No one may cross his or her arms or legs dur-ing the entire meeting. Your job is to help each other follow this new rule.** Tell teenagers that if they see anyone in the group crossing his or her arms or legs, they should simply raise both arms overhead. When students see this sign, they should make sure they're not crossing their arms or legs.

Tell teenagers that if you catch someone crossing his or her arms or legs before the rest of the group does, you'll hand that person a ribbon. If a person gets a ribbon, he or she will have the opportunity to get rid of it by helping others. For example, if the ribbon holder helps by sig-naling when someone else is crossing his or her arms or legs, by picking up someone's dropped pencil, or by getting a Bible for someone, the rib-bon will be taken back. The group goal is for you to have all the ribbons at the end of the meeting.

Number Off

OVERVIEW: Teenagers will work in teams to form number shapes with their bodies.

TIME INVOLVED: 5 to 10 minutes

SUPPLIES: a stopwatch or a watch with a second hand

PREPARATION: none

Have teenagers form two teams. Tell them that you'd like to see how well they can work together. Their task is to create with their bodies all of the number shapes from one to ten, one at a time. A team needs to use every member to create each number, and each number needs to be approved before the team can move on to the next one. When a team has finished with all ten numbers, tell them to sit down to show they're done. Before they start, ask each team:

• **How long do you think this task will take you?**

Recruit two volunteers to spot and OK the numbers while you keep time. Say: **Ready? Go!**

If one team finishes before the other team, make a mental note of that team's time. When both teams have finished, tell them their times. Then say: **Now you're going to try it again. However, this time, you'll have to do it without talking.** Then ask each team:

• **How long do you think it will take you this time?**

When teams have finished, have them give themselves a big round of applause. Point out the difference in the times, estimates, and reality with and without talking. Then ask:

• **Which way was easier? Why?**
• **What does this game tell you about working together?**
• **What role does communication play as we try to work together?**

Tag-Team Charades

OVERVIEW: Teenagers will work together in teams to guess pantomimed topics.

TIME INVOLVED: 15 to 20 minutes

SUPPLIES: paper, pens

PREPARATION: none

Have teenagers form teams of four. Give each team a piece of paper and a pen, and have each team designate a writer. Tell teams that they need to come up with as many items as they can in three categories: fast foods, book titles, and advertising slogans. Give teams a few minutes to do this, and then have them turn in their lists to you.

Then have teams scatter around the room, and explain that teams are going to play a form of Charades with the lists they just created. Here's how this will work: Each team will select someone to go first. Those people will run to you and get the topic to pantomime for their teams. For example, the first topic might be "Big Mac." Teenagers need to run back to their respective teams and pantomime the topic in such a way that their teams can guess the topic. As soon as a player's teammates guess a topic, that team chooses another player to run to you and get another topic. The object is for teams to compete to be first to guess what is being pantomimed.

When you're giving topics to teams, feel free to draw from any of the categories and lists.

Play until one team finishes. Then ask:

• **What was required to be successful at this game? Explain.**

• **What does this game tell you about the importance of good communication to working together as a group?**

Copy Cat

OVERVIEW: Teenagers will secretly imitate each other's movements.
TIME INVOLVED: 5 to 10 minutes
SUPPLIES: none
PREPARATION: none

Have teenagers stand in a circle. Explain that each person will need to secretly choose one other person in the circle to be his or her "leader." Tell teenagers not to tell anyone who their leaders are. Once the game starts, they are to try to mirror exactly every movement their leaders make. For example, if a teenager's leader crosses his or her arms, that teenager should immediately cross his or her arms as well. Explain that teenagers should try not to look at their leaders directly so that leaders won't know who is mimicking them.

Make sure teenagers understand the activity, and then have them close their eyes and open them on the count of three. As soon as their eyes are open, have them begin to follow their leaders.

Have students play for a few minutes, and then stop them and ask:

• **What was it like to try to follow someone else's movements without being noticed?**

• **What was it like to have someone following your movements?**

• **How is this experience like conforming to the "crowd" or being independent? Explain.**

Return to Childhood

OVERVIEW: Teenagers will work together to complete a children's activity book.
TIME INVOLVED: 15 to 20 minutes
SUPPLIES: two identical children's activity books, crayons
PREPARATION: none

D ivide your group into two teams. You'll need to have enough space so members of both teams can spread out and work.

Say: **Now we are going to have a little competition. The object of this little activity is to be the first team to complete a children's activity book. We have spared no expense to obtain some of the most challenging crossword puzzles, connect-the-dots pictures, and color-by-number games around.** Explain that once you've given a team a book, team members should split up the different activities so that each person can complete one activity. Have team members tear out the pages and give them to the appropriate people. Once the pages have been assigned, have teenagers work as quickly as possible to complete them. When the pages are complete, members of the team will need to put the pages back together in the original order, and stand up and sing the "Alphabet Song" as loud as they can. The first team to finish the song wins.

When teams have finished, have them sit down, and ask:

• Do you think that you could have completed the book as quickly if you had to do it on your own?

• What are some other things that we can accomplish more effectively if we work together?

Challenge the teenagers to put one of their ideas into practice. Encourage teenagers to keep their pages in visible places to remind them of the importance of working together.

I've Got a Question!

OVERVIEW: Teenagers will get to know each other better by asking and answering a variety of questions.

TIME INVOLVED: 20 to 25 minutes

SUPPLIES: pens, index cards, a hat or other container

PREPARATION: none

Have teenagers form a circle. Explain that group members are going to get to know one another better by asking and answering some questions. Give each person two index cards and a pen. Tell students to write one question on each card that will help group members get to know each other better. Tell students that because they won't know who in the group will answer each question, the questions need to be general enough that everyone could answer them. Ask students to keep the questions fairly serious and "squeaky clean." One example of a good question might be, "If you won a million dollars, what would you do with it?"

Give students a few minutes to write the questions. Screen the questions for appropriateness as the students give them to you. Remember that you will not have control over which student gets which question. Put all the questions in a hat or another container. Pass the container around the circle, and have each student pick an index card, read the question aloud, and answer the question. When everyone's answered at least one question, ask:

• Is asking and answering questions like these a good way to get to know each other? Explain.

• Which questions were the toughest to answer? Why?

• What are some of the best questions to ask someone you'd like to get to know better?

Getting to Know You...

OVERVIEW: Teenagers will discover what they have in common with other members of the group.

TIME INVOLVED: 10 to 20 minutes

SUPPLIES: paper, pens

PREPARATION: none

Give each person a piece of paper and a pen. Have students draw three vertical lines on their papers to create four columns, and write "name" on the top of the first column, "interests" on top of the second column, "likes" on top of the third column, and "dislikes" on top of the fourth column. Tell teenagers they will mingle and talk with each other to try to discover an interest, a like, and a dislike that he or she has in common with other group members. The goal is to list as many people as possible in the appropriate columns.

Give teenagers about five minutes to mingle and talk to each other. Then call them back together and ask each person to share what he or she discovered about other teenagers. Ask:

• What was the most surprising thing you heard?

• Were you surprised with how much you had in common with so many others here? Explain.

• How can what you listed on your paper become common ground for beginning or building a relationship with others in our group? Explain.

Put Your Hand on the Can, Man!

OVERVIEW: Teenagers will try to place as many appendages as possible on a pop can to illustrate the importance of each member to the group.

TIME INVOLVED: 5 to 10 minutes

69

SUPPLIES: an empty pop can for each team of five to ten students

PREPARATION: Clean out the cans.

Have group members form teams of five to ten people each, and give each team a pop can. Teams will try to get as many team members' fingertips as possible to touch the top and bottom of their team's can without touching the sides of the can. Allow teams up to thirty seconds to strategize and get their fingers positioned before you count which team has the most fingertips touching the tops and bottoms of cans. If you have small teams, have teams work to get as many fingertips as possible on only the top or the bottom of the cans. Have teams play several rounds of this game. Then ask:

• How did you feel as you worked with your team to get the most fingers on your pop can? Explain.

• How important was it to work together to succeed in this game?

• How would you describe the efforts of your team to touch the can with as many fingertips as possible? Explain.

Say: We had to work together to get everyone's fingers on the can. Everyone was important. Ask:

• How should we work together similarly to make everyone in our group feel accepted? feel important to the group?

• Why is this important?

• What are some practical ways we can do this?

Say: To be successful in this game, teams had to work hard to get all their members' fingertips on the can. To be a successful group, we must work to make everyone in our group feel accepted and important.

Ask the Answer Man!

OVERVIEW: Teenagers will work together to answer their classmates' questions.

TIME INVOLVED: 5 to 10 minutes

SUPPLIES: none

PREPARATION: none

Have teenagers form groups of four. Explain that the special guest today is the all-seeing, all-knowing "answer man" who can answer any question. Groups will take turns acting as this special guest. Choose a group to go first by determining which group has a member whose birthday is closest to today's date. Explain to the whole group that these four people will act, collectively, as the "answer man" by answering any question. However, each member of the group can say only one word at a time. The members of the "answer man" cannot confer with one another before answering a question. For example, a question might be "Will I pass my math test?" The first person might say "Not," the second person might say "on," the third person might say "your," and the fourth person might say "life." Explain that the group can come up with more than a four-word answer—the answering will just start over with the first person again.

Begin the questioning, and after the answer, have another group volunteer to go next. Continue until each group has had a chance to answer a question. Ask:

• **What did you think of this form of answering questions? Was it easy or difficult? Explain.**

• **How hard was it to predict or add on to what someone else said?**

Make a Machine

OVERVIEW: Teenagers will work together in groups to create their own "working" machines.

TIME INVOLVED: 15 to 20 minutes

SUPPLIES: none

PREPARATION: none

Have teenagers form groups of four or five. Explain that each group will have five minutes to work together to create a "working" machine. The machine can be patterned after an actual machine or can be a new invention! There are two rules to follow in creating machines:

• Each person must be a unique part of the machine.

• The machine must have a purpose that the group can explain.

71

Make sure teenagers understand the rules, and then have them begin creating their machines. While groups are working, circulate to offer ideas and suggestions.

After about five minutes, ask each group to share its machine with the rest of the groups.

When all the groups have shared, ask:

• **Was it easy or difficult to involve everyone? Explain.**

• **Why do you think it was important to involve everyone?**

• **Did you feel that everyone was an important part of the machine? Why or why not?**

Confidence Builders

I Spy

OVERVIEW: Teenagers will "spy" Christlike qualities in each other.
TIME INVOLVED: 15 to 20 minutes
SUPPLIES: none
PREPARATION: none

Have teenagers form trios, and tell them they're going to play a version of the old game "I Spy," only this time they will be spying Christlike qualities in each other. Explain that one person in each trio will be the Spy, one person will be the Guesser, and the third person will be the Subject. The Spy will choose a Christlike quality he or she has seen in the Subject. Then the Spy will give the Guesser clues until the Guesser guesses the quality. Remind teenagers that the "spied" qualities must be positive, encouraging, and true.

Have teenagers rotate roles until everyone has had a chance to play each role. Then, if teenagers are still interested, have them switch trios.

Tell Me More

OVERVIEW: Teenagers will "color" each other's good qualities.
TIME INVOLVED: 15 to 20 minutes
SUPPLIES: crayons, paper
PREPARATION: none

Give each teenager a different-colored crayon and a sheet of paper. Tell them they're going to take some time to "doodle" things that represent each other's good qualities. Give them the example of a face with two open eyes to represent someone always giving his or her full attention.

Encourage teenagers to mingle, and ask each teenager to doodle positive qualities on at least five other people's papers. As a teenager draws a doodle, have him or her explain the doodle by verbally completing this sentence: "I like the way you_____ because_____." Tell teenagers that they can't draw the same doodle more than once—they all must be different.

Give teenagers several minutes to mingle and doodle, and then have them gather back together to share what they observed about one another and discovered about themselves.

I've Been Got!

OVERVIEW: Teenagers will engage in a game that encourages them to meet the eyes of others.

TIME INVOLVED: 15 to 20 minutes

SUPPLIES: one slip of paper for each person, a marker, a small container

PREPARATION: Draw an X on one slip of paper, and then fold all the slips of paper and put them in a small container.

Have teenagers stand in a circle, and then choose an "It" by passing around the container and drawing out slips of paper. The person who draws the slip with the X is "It." Tell teenagers that "It" shouldn't reveal himself or herself.

When everyone has a slip of paper, explain the following rules. The object of the game is for "It" to eliminate everyone else by winking at them, one at a time, without being seen by anyone else. The other players' job is to try to catch "It" winking at someone without being winked at themselves. If "It" winks at a person, that person should count to five silently and then say, "I've been got!" Once a person's been "got," he or she is out of the game and should sit down.

After you've explained these rules, encourage teenagers to mingle and watch each other's eyes. After enough people have been eliminated to make the identity of "It" obvious, select a new "It" and play again.

Then ask:

• **How did it feel to make eye contact with everyone else? Explain.**

• **Why do you think making eye contact is important?**

And the Band Played On

OVERVIEW: Teenagers will enjoy making "instruments" and performing in a "band."

TIME INVOLVED: 10 to 15 minutes

SUPPLIES: various materials to make musical instruments, including rubber bands, empty tissue boxes, dried beans, aluminum pie plates, tape, combs, wax paper, drinking glasses, water, an empty bottle, empty coffee cans, paper or cloth, and pencils

PREPARATION: Set out all of the materials.

Have teenagers form groups of at least four. (If you have fewer than eight group members, let teenagers form one large group.) Explain that each group is now a band.

Let group members make instruments from the supplies you've set out. For example, dried beans inside two aluminum pie plates taped together make a "tambourine," or rubber bands stretched over an empty tissue box make a "guitar." Wax paper over a comb makes a "kazoo," and filled glasses with varying amounts of water make different sounds when tapped with a pencil. Someone may stretch paper or cloth over the top of a coffee can and use a rubber band to hold it in place to form a "drum" that can be tapped with a pencil.

When each group has constructed several instruments, have each choose a song to perform. Suggest they start out with simple songs, such as "Mary Had a Little Lamb." After a little practice, they can move on to more complicated songs. Even the most nonmusical person can be a successful musician in this kind of band!

Jump-Rope Jingle

OVERVIEW: Teenagers will play old-fashioned jump-rope.

TIME INVOLVED: 5 to 10 minutes

SUPPLIES: a six-foot length of light rope

PREPARATION: none

Turn back the clock to yesteryear (you know—before computer games) for an old-fashioned game of jump-rope. The members of your group may not have played this game since early childhood, if they even played it then.

Choose two people to be the Enders. The Enders turn the rope for the other members of the group. As the Enders turn the rope at a steady pace, let each group member jump for an appointed time. The easiest way to time jumpers is by using a jump-rope rhyme.

Here are a few rhymes to get you started. Have one group member begin jumping as you say: **Polly put the kettle on, kettle on, kettle on. Polly put the kettle on, and in came** (name of the second jumper). The first jumper jumps out as the second jumper jumps in and repeats the rhyme, naming a third jumper at the end of the rhyme.

Here's another simple rhyme: One person jumps as you say: **I like coffee. I like tea. I like** (name of second jumper), **and** (name of second jumper) **likes me.** The first jumper jumps out as the second jumper jumps in and repeats the rhyme, naming the third jumper.

For a more challenging game, let someone call, "Salt and pepper!" The Enders will turn the rope as fast as possible until the jumper misses a beat.

Make sure to rotate players so the Enders get a chance to jump. You'll be amazed at the workout this game provides!

Yearbook Signing Party

OVERVIEW: Teenagers will gain confidence as they receive encouraging notes from each other.

TIME INVOLVED: 15 to 30 minutes

SUPPLIES: a CD or cassette player with a CD or cassette tape of fun background music, paper, yarn, scissors, markers

PREPARATION: Fold several pieces of paper into a "yearbook" and tie the binding with a piece of yarn (see diagram on page 78). You'll need one yearbook for each student.

Have teenagers sit in a circle. Then say: **Everyone loves it when yearbooks come out. We not only love looking at the pictures, but we love getting our yearbooks signed. We try to summarize the year and our feelings for each person in a short little paragraph. Wouldn't it be nice to get those encouraging notes more than once a year? Well, today we're going to have an early year-book signing party.**

Hand out the yearbooks and markers.

Say: **Take a few minutes to decorate the front cover of your yearbook. Be sure your name is on it.**

Give teenagers a few minutes to do this and then explain that the yearbook signing will resemble Musical Chairs. When the music is playing, teenagers will pass the yearbooks around the circle. When the music stops, each teenager will need to write an encouraging note to the person whose yearbook he or she is holding. Each time you stop the music, give teenagers about a minute to sign the yearbooks. Tell them that if they get a yearbook they've already signed, they should write another encouraging note to the same person. If teenagers get their own yearbook, they should write a brief encouraging note to themselves.

Have teenagers take their yearbooks home with them and hang them where they'll see them often.

Problem Toss

OVERVIEW: Teenagers will have the opportunity to throw their difficult questions into a basket and then have those questions answered.

TIME INVOLVED: 1 hour

SUPPLIES: paper, pens, and a wastebasket

PREPARATION: none

G ive each teenager a sheet of paper and a pen, and have them write down one question they've struggled with during the past six months. Tell them not to put their names on their papers.

Once everyone has written down a question, place a wastebasket in the center of the room and tell teenagers to crumple up their questions and toss them into the basket.

Then have the large group divide into groups of four, and give each group four crumpled questions and a clean sheet of paper. Tell groups that their job is to come up with some possible solutions for the questions they've been given. Allow groups about twenty minutes to answer their questions.

Come back together as a large group, and have each group read its questions and answers out loud so that each question's writer will gain his or her peers' insight.

Who Am I?

OVERVIEW: Teenagers will build confidence in their knowledge of the Bible as they work together to guess Bible characters.

TIME INVOLVED: 20 to 30 minutes

SUPPLIES: index cards, pens

PREPARATION: Write the names of various Bible characters on index cards. Make sure that teenagers will be able to identify the characters you choose.

G ive each person an index card with a Bible character's name on it and a pen. Tell teenagers not to show anyone the name on their cards. Explain that the other members of the group are going to work together to guess each person's Bible character. To help them, each person will need to write everything he or she knows about the Bible character on the back of the index card. For example, if a person's Bible character is Mary, that person can write, "She's Jesus' mother" on the back of the card.

Give teenagers a few minutes to do this. If someone is having trouble, take that person aside and help him or her find the character in the Bible.

When teenagers are finished, choose one person to go first. Say: **Now you need to give us clues about your character so that we can**

79

guess who it is. Use the information on the back of your index card, and give us one clue at a time. Let's see how many clues it takes us.

Continue in this manner until every Bible character has been guessed. Then lead a short discussion. Ask:

• How well do you do at giving others clues as to who you are?

• Do you feel other people know the real you? Explain.

• What can you do to help others get to know you?

• What is one thing that is most important for others to know about you?

Say: We need to give others more of an opportunity to know us.

Stand-Up Show and Tell

OVERVIEW: Teenagers will Show and Tell about items they're wearing or that they have brought with them.

TIME INVOLVED: 20 to 30 minutes

SUPPLIES: none

PREPARATION: none

Tell teenagers that they're going to do an activity they all knew and loved when they were younger—Show and Tell.

Have teenagers choose something they are wearing or something they have brought to class. Explain that you'd like teenagers to think about why the items they chose are special to them or are part of their identities. For example, someone may share about a cross necklace that belonged to a grandmother. Another may explain that a T-shirt depicts a favorite singing group or color.

Then ask teenagers to Show and Tell one at a time.

Encourage other group members to ask questions, and give everyone a chance to present.

Etiquette Antics

OVERVIEW: Teenagers will have fun acting out various scenarios requiring knowledge of proper etiquette.

TIME INVOLVED: 15 to 30 minutes

SUPPLIES: a reference book about proper etiquette and social graces, such as *Dear Ms. Demeanor: The Young Person's Etiquette Guide to Handling Any Social Situation With Confidence and Grace* (Contemporary Publishing, 1995); a pen; paper; etiquette props, such as a toy telephone, dinner napkins, tableware, glasses, a pitcher, assorted snack foods (optional)

PREPARATION: Find several important rules of etiquette in the etiquette reference book that teenagers can act out. Mark the pages so you can find them easily later. Then write each scenario on a slip of paper, and assemble any needed props. For example, one rule of etiquette may address the proper way to answer the telephone and take a message. Write this scenario on a slip of paper and provide a toy telephone. Other possible scenarios to write out may include the proper way to seat a lady at a table, the proper way to use a napkin, the proper way to serve and pass food, the proper way to pour beverages, and the proper way to introduce and greet someone. Set out the props.

Have teenagers form pairs or trios. Ask:
 • How do you rate your manners—excellent, average, or barbaric? Why?

Say: **Today we're going to have some fun learning about the "proper" ways of doing certain things. I'm going to give each group a rule of etiquette on a slip of paper. I'd like you to read your rule and then take about five minutes to decide how to demonstrate it to the rest of the group. Use the props if you'd like.** Give groups five minutes to plan their skits and then ask one group to come forward and act it out. When the group is finished, have the other groups vote on whether or not the group demonstrated proper etiquette in the situation. After the whole group has voted, read a short description from the etiquette book about the proper way to handle the situation. Continue in this manner until all rules have been presented and voted on. Then ask:

 • **Why is it important to know and practice good manners?**

Cereal Box Self-Portraits

OVERVIEW: Teenagers will use empty cereal boxes to describe their finest "selling" points as Christians.

TIME INVOLVED: 20 to 30 minutes

SUPPLIES: an empty cereal box for each person; scissors; markers; construction paper; glue; assorted cereal, milk, bowls, spoons (optional)

PREPARATION: Read through the activity and then create your own cereal box self-portrait as a sample. Set out the materials.

Give each person a cereal box. Say: **I'd like you each to spend a few minutes thinking about the character qualities and gifts which God has given you that might be viewed as "selling points" for Christianity. For example, you may be trustworthy, kind, gentle, faithful, loving, meek, courteous, brave, honest, or forgiving. Then I'd like you to use your cereal box and the supplies provided to demonstrate the hottest, best-selling new product on the market today—you. Use your character qualities and gifts as the advertising points.**

Suggest that teenagers use the colorful advertising already on the box. They may also want to use construction paper to cover over some words in order to supply their own funny and appealing promises. Encourage teenagers to redo all four sides of their cereal boxes.

When the boxes are completed, have teenagers take turns presenting them to the group.

If you'd like, provide a cereal snack.

Slap 'n' Clap

OVERVIEW: Teenagers will receive standing ovations.

TIME INVOLVED: 5 to 10 minutes

SUPPLIES: none

PREPARATION: none

H ave teenagers stand shoulder to shoulder, facing in one direction. Have each person hold out his or her right hand, palm up. Explain that the first person in line will run back and forth down the line, slapping the hands of others along the way. Once a person's hand has been slapped, that person will start applauding the runner and cheering him or her on. When the runner returns to the starting point, the next person in line becomes the new runner.

Continue until everyone has had the chance to run, slap, and be presented with a standing ovation by his or her peers.

Meet and Greet

OVERVIEW: Teenagers will find their groups by gum flavor, then share something special about each other.

TIME INVOLVED: 5 to 10 minutes

SUPPLIES: four different flavors of gum, a bowl

PREPARATION: Open the packages of gum and mix the pieces in the bowl. Make sure there is just one piece of gum for each person.

H ave teenagers each choose a piece of gum. Let them know that they can chew the gum, but they need to keep the wrappers.

Read Psalm 139:13-16 aloud and ask:

• **How does this passage make you feel?**

Say: **God made each one of us special. Now I'd like you to share with a small group how each person was made special.**

Have teenagers find the other people who are chewing their flavor of gum. When groups have formed, have them sit in a circle. Say: **Now each person in your group needs to think of something positive to say about every other person. Begin each sentence about a person by saying, "God made you special by" and then finish the sentence. For example, someone might say, "God made you special by giving you a wonderful singing voice."**

Chasing the Crown

OVERVIEW: Teenagers will race to a chair.

TIME INVOLVED: 15 to 30 minutes

SUPPLIES: several decks of cards, a chair

PREPARATION: none

Have teenagers form groups of four to eight. Direct each group to a different part of the room, and have each group sit in a circle. Place a deck of cards in the middle of each circle, and place the chair at a point that is roughly the same distance from each circle. Have one person in each circle shuffle the cards and lay them face down in the center. Tell group members that they are to take turns turning the top card over every time you say: **Turn.**

If the card turned is an ace, king, queen, or jack, the person who turned it grabs the card, stands up, and runs to touch the chair and return to his or her circle. If another group has a runner at the same time, it becomes a race. The first person to touch the chair gets to keep all the other people who got up to run; those people join the winner's circle.

The group with the most people in their circle at the end of the playing time wins.

Superheroes

OVERVIEW: Groups will create superheroes based on group members' strengths. Then they will address challenges.

TIME INVOLVED: 15 to 20 minutes

SUPPLIES: none

PREPARATION: none

Have teenagers line up according to birthdays—people with January birthdays first, then people with February birthdays, and so on. Then have the first four teenagers form a group, the second four form a group, and so on.

Say: **Each person in your group is special and has unique and important strengths. Your group's first job is to think of each group** member's most outstanding strength that's not related to appearance. For example, someone in your group may be a good runner, or a history buff, or a good listener.

After groups have thought of strengths, have them each create a superhero whose powers reflect all the group members' strengths—for instance, a superhero who can run faster than a car, strategize according to historical examples, and hear a pin drop a mile away. Then have groups take turns introducing their superheroes to the other groups, including the group member's characteristics that each superhero represents.

Then describe a challenge that a typical superhero might have to address—an evildoer who can shoot lightning bolts is robbing a bank, for example—and give each group one minute to name a way its superhero could face that challenge.

Play several rounds, describing other challenges—a space shuttle that's headed the wrong direction, a giant dinosaur that's terrorizing a city, a mad scientist who's planning to destroy the sun. Afterward, lead a discussion on the importance of the diversity of people's strengths.

"Greatest Achievement" Night

OVERVIEW: Teenagers each have the opportunity to be the center of attention for part of the meeting time.

TIME INVOLVED: 2 hours

SUPPLIES: "Certificate of Achievement" handout (p. 87), pens, tape

PREPARATION: Make enough copies of the "Certificate of Achievement" handout (p. 87) for each person.

Give each person a "Certificate of Achievement," and have them each fill in their greatest achievements. Tell teenagers not to show their certificates to anyone else. When teenagers are finished, collect the certificates and say: **Now we're going to have a little fun trying to guess what each person's greatest achievement is. I'll read an achievement, and then we'll take a vote to decide as a group who the achievement belongs to. Afterward we'll find out if we guessed right.**

Once the vote has been taken and the achiever's identity has been revealed, have that person tell the group a bit more about his or her achievement. Continue in this manner until everyone has been recognized.

Then have teenagers help each other tape their certificates to their backs, and have them sign each other's awards and verbally affirm each other.

Personal Trading Cards

OVERVIEW: Teenagers will create trading cards for each other.

TIME INVOLVED: 20 to 30 minutes

SUPPLIES: several instant-print cameras with film, glue sticks, paper squares, scissors, pens

PREPARATION: Cut paper into squares that are the same size as the instant-print pictures.

Have teenagers form groups of four to six, and give each group an instant-print camera, paper squares, and pens. Say: **Today we're going to focus on each other's strengths and good points. To do this, we're going to create trading cards about ourselves for each other, you know, like baseball trading cards. In your group, take turns taking each other's pictures. Each group member will need to have a photo of himself or herself.**

Give groups a few minutes to do this. Then say: **Now you'll need to glue a paper square on the back of your picture. When you've done this, pass around your pictures. Each person in your group should write something positive about each other person on the back of the pictures.**

The Pizza Plan

OVERVIEW: Teenagers will work in teams to create a plan.

TIME INVOLVED: 20 to 30 minutes

Certificate of Achievement

You're the Greatest

We're glad you're part of our group

_____

Greatest Achievement

SUPPLIES: paper, pens, ingredients to make pizza (optional)
PREPARATION: none

Have teenagers form groups of three or four. Give each group one sheet of paper and a pen. Ask:

• Do you all like pizza? What do you like on your pizza?

Say: Today you're going to create a plan for making the best pizza ever. Each group will write "how-to" instructions for making pizza. You'll need to begin at the beginning, and be sure you don't leave any steps out. Pretend I'm an alien from another planet, and I have no idea how to make a pizza. Tell me everything I need to do!

Have members of each group work together to write step-by-step directions for making a pizza. When groups are finished, have each group appoint a Head Chef to share the group's recipe with the whole group. (No editing is allowed once the recipe reading begins.)

It's very likely that groups will overlook the most obvious issues, such as going to the grocery store to buy ingredients, turning on the oven, or putting the ingredients onto a pizza pan.

For a laugh, let the group decipher exactly what kind of mess each set of directions would render. For example, a group might end up with ingredients splattered all over the table because they forgot a bowl. Another group might have a pizza sitting in an oven that was never turned on.

Decide which group came the closest to making an edible pizza.

For added fun, provide pizza ingredients and let groups make, bake, and eat their own pizzas.

Jesus Loves Me

OVERVIEW: Teenagers will help to write new words to an old tune.
TIME INVOLVED: 15 to 20 minutes
SUPPLIES: "Jesus Loves Me" handout (p. 90), paper, pens
PREPARATION: Make enough copies of the "Jesus Loves Me" handout for each team to have one.

Have teenagers form teams of four or five. Give each team paper, pens and a "Jesus Loves Me" handout. Have teams sing "Jesus

Loves Me" together.

Then tell teams that their job is to rewrite the words to the song using the same tune. Each team member should contribute at least one phrase, and the words can be anything about God! Give teams five minutes to come up with their new versions of the song.

When teams are finished, ask each team to perform its new song. End with lots of applause for all teams' efforts!

String of Affirmation

OVERVIEW: Teenagers will affirm each other as they toss a ball of string around.

TIME INVOLVED: 20 to 25 minutes

SUPPLIES: ball of string or yarn

PREPARATION: none

Have group members stand or sit in a circle. Holding the ball of string, say: **The Bible makes it clear that we should "encourage one another daily"** (Hebrews 3:13). **When is the last time you encouraged someone in this room? Well, you're about to get an opportunity to encourage everyone.** Explain that the first person will toss the ball of string to someone else in the group while holding on to the end of the string. After the first person throws the ball, he or she will say two encouraging things about the person who catches the string. For example, the first person might say, "You're always kind to everyone" and "I really enjoy your friendship." Then the person who received the ball of string will throw it to someone else as he or she holds on to part of the string and say two encouraging things about that person.

Continue to pass the ball of string until everyone in the group is holding a part of the string. Ask:

• **How does this web of string represent encouragement within our group?**

• **How can our group make it a practice to encourage each other?**

You can hang up the web of string as a reminder of how your group should be connected and of the importance of encouragement.

Jesus Loves Me

Jesus loves me! this I know,
For the Bible tells me so;
Little ones to him belong,
They are weak but he is strong.

Yes, Jesus loves me!
Yes, Jesus loves me!
Yes, Jesus loves me!
The Bible tells me so.

Not-So-Random Acts of Kindness

OVERVIEW: Teenagers will visit two or three people around the church and treat them to numerous acts of kindness.

TIME INVOLVED: 20 to 30 minutes

SUPPLIES: various items to show kindness, including pillows, bubbles, balloons, noisemakers, cardboard crowns, and craft supplies to make homemade cards

PREPARATION: Go to two or three leaders in the church who lead classes or groups at the same time you meet with the youth. Ask these leaders each to recommend one person in the class or group who could use some extra encouragement or a pat on the back. These people will be your "targets" for your "not-so-random acts of kindness."

Begin by letting teenagers know that all of you will be showing some extra kindness and encouragement to certain people. Let the group know who you'll be visiting and why. Then have teenagers come up with a plan to show kindness to these people. Some suggestions include:

- blowing noisemakers,
- cheering (with an original cheer),
- clapping and whistling,
- placing a cardboard crown on the person's head,
- propping the person's feet up on a pillow,
- giving the person a neck and shoulder massage,
- giving the person balloons,
- giving the person a homemade affirmation card, or
- carrying the person around on group members' shoulders.

After visiting each of your targets, have the group return to your room. Ask:

- **How did it feel to express kindness and encouragement to others? Why?**

- **Were you surprised by the recipients' reactions? Why? How do you think they felt?**

• Why do you think it is so important for us to be kind and encouraging to one another?

• What can we do to be kinder and more encouraging to one another?

Pat on the Back

OVERVIEW: Teenagers will gain confidence as they share what they like about themselves.

TIME INVOLVED: 5 to 10 minutes

SUPPLIES: none

PREPARATION: none

Have teenagers form pairs, and tell them that they're going to give themselves a "pat on the back." Explain that partners will have thirty seconds to tell each other everything they like about themselves. For example, one partner might begin by saying "I'm kind to everyone." The partner's job is to listen carefully and supportively, as well as counting aloud the positive things his or her partner says.

After thirty seconds, have partners switch roles.

After time is up, ask volunteers to share how many positive things they or their partners came up with. Encourage volunteers to share a few of the positive things. Ask:

• Was this exercise easy or difficult? Why?

• Have you ever heard the saying, "I am my own worst critic"? How do you feel about that?

• Why do you think we tend to focus on our own negative qualities rather than the positive ones?

• Why is it important to remember our good qualities?

Encourage teenagers to remember the good qualities, both the ones they heard and the ones they listed. When they're feeling down, have them remind themselves and each other of what special people they are!

Tell Me a Story!

OVERVIEW: Teenagers will make presentations about various topics while the group practices good listening.

TIME INVOLVED: 15 to 20 minutes

SUPPLIES: newsprint or a dry-erase board and a marker

PREPARATION: Write the following topics on the newsprint or the dry-erase board:

- Incredible coincidences
- Scientific wonders
- Personal stories
- Hilarious and true
- Embarrassing episodes
- Clean joke of the day
- Strange and true

Explain to teenagers that they're all going to have a chance to share something with the group. Point out the categories on the newsprint, and tell teenagers that they can choose one of the categories for something to share with the rest of the group. Tell teenagers that they don't have to share—participation in this activity is on a volunteer basis only. However, all students will be involved as the audience.

Give teenagers a minute to think about the categories, and then ask a volunteer to go first. Explain that the person has up to one minute to share a story or joke, while the rest of the group listens politely. While the student is presenting, take mental note of some of the highlights or important points of the presentation. When the first volunteer is finished, lead the rest of the group in a round of applause.

Allow all volunteers to share, continuing to make mental notes on each one. When everyone who wants to has shared, challenge students to recall as many things as possible from each person's presentation. Then ask:

• Presenters, how did it feel to tell your story?

• Audience members, did you remember lots or not very much about everyone's presentations?

• Do you think you're a good listener? Rank yourself on a scale from one to ten, with one being low. Why did you rank yourself where you did?

• Why is it important to be a good listener?

• What does it take to be a good listener?

Faith Builders

Armor of God

OVERVIEW: Teenagers will recognize the value of the armor of God.
TIME INVOLVED: 10 to 15 minutes
SUPPLIES: Bibles, paper, pens
PREPARATION: none

Read Ephesians 6:10-18. Say: **In this passage, the Apostle Paul explains to the Ephesians the armor that Christ has provided** for doing battle with the devil. Four items included in this armor are a breastplate, a shield, a helmet, and a sword. I'd like you to think about the ways these items are meant to protect us as Christians.

Have teenagers form pairs, and give each pair a Bible, a pen, and a sheet of paper. Say: **I'd like you to write each item on your sheet of paper: the breastplate of righteousness, the shield of faith, the helmet of salvation, and the sword of the Spirit. Then, with your partner, I'd like you to think about all the ways each item might protect you. List those ways under the item. For example, you might say that the breastplate of righteousness will keep you safe from temptations or that the shield of the Spirit gives you the strength to speak your beliefs or stand up for someone being ridiculed for his or her beliefs.**

Tally up the lists and see which pair is "best-dressed" for battle. Have pairs share their answers with each other.

Pass the Hat

OVERVIEW: Teenagers will discover that respect can be faith-affirming.
TIME INVOLVED: 10 to 30 minutes
SUPPLIES: a Bible, various hats
PREPARATION: Decide beforehand which hat will be the special hat.

Have teenagers sit in a circle, and read Philemon 6–7 aloud. Ask:
• **What do these verses tell us about the way we should treat each other? Why do you think this is important?**

Give each person a hat, and say: **Now I'd like everyone to wear a** hat. One is special. Whoever is wearing that hat must sit in the mid-

hat. One is special. Whoever is wearing that hat must sit in the middle of the circle. Each person in the group will then offer a positive thought or word of affirmation for the person in the middle. When we say positive words to each other, we're not only encouraging and sharing God's love with each other, we're also sharing our faith. Tell which hat is the special hat and then have the person wearing that hat sit in the middle.

After everyone has offered positive thoughts or words of affirmation, have teenagers take off their hats and pass them to the right. Have them continue to pass the hats until you say "stop." Then each person puts on the hat he or she is holding. Whoever is wearing the special hat goes to the center of the circle, and the process is repeated. Continue in this manner until everyone has sat in the middle of the circle.

Christmas Cheer

OVERVIEW: Teenagers will work together to "tell" the different versions of the Christmas story through Charades.

TIME INVOLVED: 20 to 30 minutes

SUPPLIES: Bibles, simple costumes (optional)

PREPARATION: none

Divide teenagers into two teams, and give each team Bibles and costumes if you have them. Then say: **First, I'd like each team to read the story of Jesus' birth. One team will read the story found in Luke 2:1-20, and the other will read the story in Matthew 2. Then each team will produce a sequence of five or six charade scenes to present the elements of your story. The goal is to "tell" your version of the Christmas story (through Charades) in the shortest possible time.**

As needed, help each team with the various elements of the story. When teams have finished planning their charades, have them take turns presenting their charades to each other. This game offers a wonderful opportunity for a discussion of the Christmas story or a devotion about the birth of Jesus.

I've Got a Secret to Share

OVERVIEW: Teenagers will share the teachings of Jesus with each other by passing his words along to others.

TIME INVOLVED: 10 to 15 minutes

SUPPLIES: a Bible

PREPARATION: Select several short phrases from the Sermon on the Mount (Matthew 5–7).

This game is played much like Telephone.

Have teenagers sit in a circle on the floor. Then say: **I've got a secret, and I'd like to pass it along to the others. I'll whisper my secret into the ear of the first person in the circle, then he or she will whisper my secret into the next person's ear, and so on around the circle. The last person will whisper the secret into my ear.**

Begin by whispering one of your chosen phrases, such as "You are the salt of the earth."

Each time, after the secret has made the round of the circle, read aloud the teaching from the Bible.

Ask:

- **What does this teaching mean?**
- **Why is it important to tell about the teachings of Jesus correctly?**
- **What are some ways we can share Jesus' teachings with others?**

Family Tree

OVERVIEW: Teenagers will work to reconstruct the genealogy of Jesus as found in Matthew 1.

TIME INVOLVED: 10 to 15 minutes

SUPPLIES: Bibles, index cards, pens

PREPARATION: Before the meeting, write a number of the more prominent names from the genealogy of Jesus in Matthew 1 on individual index cards. For example, cards might include Abraham, Isaac, David, and Solomon. Make one set of cards for each team of four.

H ave teenagers form teams of four, and give each team Bibles, two cards, and pens.

Read Matthew 1 aloud and have teenagers follow along while you read. When you're finished, ask:

• Why is the information in this passage important?

Say: **This information is important because it shows us where Jesus came from. The people included in this genealogy are people who God chose to do his work through history. Now let's see how much we know about some of these people. In your teams, I'd like you to look through your cards and write down any information you may remember about these people on the back of the cards. Some people may seem kind of obscure, while others will be better known. You have ten minutes to write down as much information as you can. You may use your Bibles to help you. Let's see which team can find the most facts about the most people.**

After teams have filled in their cards, ask them to present what they wrote. Then discuss some of the people mentioned in the genealogy and why they were important to God's work or why it might have been important to include them in the genealogy.

Lights Out!

OVERVIEW: Teenagers will discover what it might be like to be blind, both physically and spiritually.

TIME INVOLVED: 15 to 20 minutes

SUPPLIES: a Bible

PREPARATION: Find a room that becomes totally dark when the lights are turned off.

H ave teenagers stand in one corner of the room with their eyes closed. Say: **In a moment, I'm going to turn out the light. When I turn it back on, there will be something different about the room. Let's see who can detect the difference.**

Turn off the light and then quickly change something in the room. You might move a lamp, turn a book upside down, or take a poster off the wall. Make noises or other distractions to keep teenagers from figuring out what you're changing. When you finish, turn the light back on and see if anyone can tell what you've changed. Play the game several times, changing different things each time. If you'd like, let volunteers change items.

Following this game, tell the story of Jesus healing the blind man (John 9). Close by reading aloud John 9:39-41. Then ask:

• **What changes did you discover each time you could see?**

• **How are these changes similar to our everyday experiences with seeing God's light?**

• **What do you think often inhibits our judgments of truth?**

• **Why is it often difficult to see God's work in the world around us?**

• **How may we be spiritually blind?**

In Your Own Words

OVERVIEW: Teenagers will paraphrase Scripture passages.

TIME INVOLVED: 5 to 10 minutes

SUPPLIES: Bibles, Bible dictionaries or other reference books, concordances, paper, pens

PREPARATION: none

Have teenagers form groups of three or four.

Give each group a Bible, a Bible dictionary or other reference book, a concordance, paper, and pens. Assign each group the same Scripture reference, and explain that they'll have five minutes to translate the reference into their own words. After five minutes, ask each group read its paraphrase. Then discuss similarities and differences in interpretation.

After this discussion, assign each group a different Scripture reference. This game is a wonderful tool to assess learning and retention of material you've taught.

Simple Sermons

OVERVIEW: Teenagers will write and present their own sermons.

TIME INVOLVED: 5 to 15 minutes

SUPPLIES: Bibles, Bible commentaries, paper, and pens

PREPARATION: none

Have teenagers form groups of four. Give each group a Bible, Bible commentary, paper, and pens. Explain that each group is to write a five-minute sermon on a topic or Scripture passage you assign. Provide students with this simple outline: introduction to the theme, brief explanation of the theme, and application of the theme.

After five minutes, a representative from each group will read the group's sermon to the rest of the class. Tell group members that each sermon must contain at least three supporting Scripture references.

You may want to assign each group a separate topic or passage, depending on your feelings about the current needs of your youth. You may even consider using this game as an ongoing weekly assignment and have teenagers present one five-minute sermon per week.

Prayer and Praise Wall

OVERVIEW: Teenagers will record prayer requests, prayers answered, and praises on a bulletin board.

TIME INVOLVED: 5 minutes at each meeting

SUPPLIES: a Bible, paper, pens, tape or tacks, a bulletin board or large section of bare wall

PREPARATION: Write "Prayer: Requests and Praises" on the top of the wall or bulletin board. On a table near the wall, leave paper, pens, and tape or tacks.

Ask:

• Tell some ways you talk to God.

• Are you satisfied with your communication with God? Is there anything you would change? If so, what?

• What was the last thing you requested of God?

• Do you feel that God answered your prayer? Explain.

• What are some other purposes for prayer besides asking God to meet our needs?

Read Mark 11:24 aloud and ask:

• What do you think this verse means?

Say: **God says that he will answer our prayers. It builds our faith to know that God truly does answer prayers. For the next month or so, we're going to keep track of our requests and God's answers.**

Hand out slips of paper and pens.

Say: **Write your prayer requests on these slips of paper, and hang them on the wall. You can fold them if you'd rather people not read them.**

Give teenagers time to write their prayers and hang them on the bulletin board or wall.

Say: **Every week, I want you to look at your prayer requests. When they are answered, write the answer next to your request. If they aren't answered, remember to continue to pray. It will be exciting to see how God is working in our lives.**

Legal Defense

OVERVIEW: Teenagers will argue for or against the Resurrection.

TIME INVOLVED: I hour

SUPPLIES: Bibles, Bible commentaries and other reference materials, paper, pens, a black robe and a gavel (optional)

PREPARATION: Set up the room to look like a courtroom. Be sure to include the jury gallery, the judge's bench, and tables for the defense and the prosecution. Have paper, pens, Bibles, and Bible commentaries and other reference materials on hand to help each group prepare its portion of the courtroom experience. Prepare a list of Scripture passages related to the Resurrection, such as Matthew 27–28; Mark 15–16; Luke 23–24; and John 19–20.

Have teenagers form three groups—a defense team, a prosecution team, and a jury. Tell the defense and the prosecution that they'll have half an hour to prepare their case about whether Christ really rose from the dead. The prosecution will try to prove that Christ didn't rise from the dead; the defense will maintain that he did rise from the dead.

Put the prosecution and defense groups in separate rooms to prepare their cases. While they're gone, have the jury develop questions that the prosecution and defense will need to answer in order to persuade them.

At the end of the thirty-minute preparation time, bring all the groups into the "courtroom" and proceed with the hearing. Make it as realistic as possible—wear a black robe and declare the court in session by pounding a gavel. Have the prosecution present its case; then the defense. Let each group present a closing argument.

Then send the jury out to determine the verdict. Discuss the experience with the other two groups while the jury is out. Then bring the jury in to hand down its verdict.

Discuss whether teenagers could have changed anything to strengthen the case for or against the Resurrection.

What Kind of Church Are We?

OVERVIEW: Teenagers will determine which of the Revelation churches they as a group most resemble.

TIME INVOLVED: 45 minutes

SUPPLIES: Bibles, Bible commentaries and other reference materials, seven pieces of poster board, markers, tape or tacks

PREPARATION: Read through Revelation 2–3 and write the names of the seven churches on pieces of poster board, one church on each piece. Hang the posters around the room.

Have teenagers form seven groups (a group can be one person). Assign each group the task of studying one of the churches on the posters and then preparing short phrases to describe the church to the whole group. Provide Bibles and Bible commentaries, and tell groups that their research needs to begin by reading about their assigned churches in Revelation 2–3.

Once groups have finished their research, have members of each group pantomime their church's characteristics for the other groups to guess.

faith builders

103

Convene the whole group for a discussion of which of the seven churches they feel the youth group most resembles. Pray as a group for ways to grow and overcome the group's shortcomings.

Prayer Webs

OVERVIEW: Teenagers will build prayer webs of support for people in distant places.

TIME INVOLVED: 20 to 30 minutes

SUPPLIES: a Bible, a basketball, pens, paper, current newspapers and news magazines

PREPARATION: none

Say: Let's make a web. Here's how we'll do it. I'd like you to stand in two lines facing each other. Cross your left arm over your right arm and grab the hands of the person across from you.

When teenagers have done this, say: Now I'm going to toss the basketball onto your web. Let's see if you can support it. Toss the basketball onto teenagers' arms. They must not drop the ball. Say: Now let's see if you can pass the ball from one end to the other and back.

When teenagers have done this, ask:

• What was the most important thing to remember as you did this?

Say: You wouldn't have been able to accomplish this task if you hadn't supported each other and worked together. Let's see what God's Word has to say about that. Read Galatians 6:2 aloud, and ask:

• What are some ways we can carry each other's burdens?

• How can we carry the burdens of people we don't know or those who are far away from us?

Say: One way God wants us to carry each other's burdens is by upholding each other in a web of prayer, just like the web of hands we created today. Now I'd like you to look through the newspapers and news magazines here to find people in crisis whose burdens you may carry through your prayer. Jot down any information you'd like to remember and then commit to praying for those people.

Toe the Line

OVERVIEW: Teenagers will walk tiptoe across a masking tape line, supported by the fingertips of others.

TIME INVOLVED: 5 to 10 minutes

SUPPLIES: masking tape, a whistle, a stopwatch or a watch with a second hand

PREPARATION: Create a masking tape line fifteen to twenty feet long on the floor in the center of the room.

Have teenagers form two groups. Ask the groups to stand side by side on either side of the tape line. Have everyone take three steps back. Explain that the first person in one line—you choose which line—is going to walk tiptoe down the tape line as quickly as possible without stepping off the tape. If a person steps off with either foot at any time, you blow the whistle and have the player return to the line. Record the time it takes the first player to walk the line successfully. Repeat the process with the other people in each line, giving everyone a chance to beat the fastest time.

Then play the game again and have each player extend both arms to the side with the index fingers pointing out. Have the people standing in the lines each extend one arm with the index finger pointing out to support the player walking down the line. As before, the goal is to try to walk the tape line as fast as possible without stepping off. Record the time it takes each player to walk the line successfully. When everyone has walked the line, have group members sit facing each other across the line. Ask:

• **How did you feel when you successfully reached the end of the line?**

• **How did it feel when you stepped off along the way?**

• **Which do you think was more important, walking the line as quickly as possible or walking the line without stepping off the tape? Why?**

• **Which was easier, crossing the line by yourself or crossing the line with support from others? Explain.**

Read James 1:2-8 aloud, and say: **Faith is often deepened by the perseverance a person needs to get through a tough time. People** often want to rush through life without considering the consequences. However, when we walk by faith, we will find added strength, often through the support of others.

Two-Minute Dramas

OVERVIEW: Teenagers will create two-minute dramas using three phrases.

TIME INVOLVED: 10 to 20 minutes

SUPPLIES: a Bible, chalkboard and chalk

PREPARATION: Write the following three phrases on the chalkboard: "Go into the world…," "Let your light shine…," and "And you shall receive power…"

Divide the group into drama teams of four or five. Direct their attention to the chalkboard. Ask the teams to read the phrases out loud. Say: **I'm going to give you five minutes to create a drama in your drama team. Your drama must be two minutes or less in length, and it should include each of the three phrases in a creative way.**

After five minutes, let each team perform its drama for the group. When all of the dramas have been performed, read Matthew 5:14-16 and 28:18-20 aloud and discuss the meaning of each of the phrases. Use examples, if you can, from the dramas the group has just seen and performed.

Bandage Relay

OVERVIEW: Teenagers will run a relay race to bandage a "hurt victim."

TIME INVOLVED: 15 to 20 minutes

SUPPLIES: a Bible, four Ace bandages per team

PREPARATION: none

Use this game to help kids connect with the story of the Good Samaritan.

Read the story of the Good Samaritan (Luke 10:25-37) aloud. Then have teenagers form teams of five. Say: **Now you're going to run a Good Samaritan relay race. Choose one of your team members to play the Victim. The other team members will be Good Samaritans.**

Have the Victims lie down about fifteen feet away from their Good Samaritans. Then place the Ace bandages (four for each team) about halfway between the Good Samaritans and the Victims.

Say: **When I say "go," one Good Samaritan from each team runs to the pile of bandages, takes one, and runs to the Victim. Then the Good Samaritan loosely wraps the bandage around the Victim and runs back to the team. When the first person returns, the next Good Samaritan does the same thing. Continue in this way until all Good Samaritans have wrapped bandages around the Victim. When the last Good Samaritan returns, all four Good Samaritans must run to the Victim and carry him or her back to the starting line. The first team to have all five of its members at the starting line wins. Ready? Go!**

Making Waves

OVERVIEW: Teenagers will make waves in a swimming pool to knock others off an air mattress.

TIME INVOLVED: 10 to 15 minutes

SUPPLIES: a Bible, a swimming pool, an air mattress

PREPARATION: none

Use this game to interject some faith-building into a pool party. Have each person take a turn sitting on an air mattress in the middle of the pool. The rest of the group should kick water with their feet, push water with their hands, or do cannonballs close to (but not on) the air mattress to create waves to knock the person off. If you'd like, you can time teenagers to see how long each person can stay on the mattress.

Afterward, lead a brief discussion about mature faith. Read aloud Ephesians 4:14-15. Ask:

• **How are the waves we created like the waves in verse 14?**

• **What are some "waves" you face in your life?**

• **How can Jesus help you deal with those waves? How can you help each other deal with those waves?**

Sightless Sandwiches

OVERVIEW: Teenagers will try to make sandwiches behind their backs.

TIME INVOLVED: 10 to 15 minutes

SUPPLIES: a Bible, bread, peanut butter, jelly, napkins, knives

PREPARATION: Set up a few sandwich-making stations, leaving room between them.

Have teenagers form as many teams as you have sandwich-making stations. Have each team gather around a station and choose a person to go first. Explain that each person is going to take a turn standing with his or her back to the supplies and try to make a peanut butter and jelly sandwich in one minute. Be sure the bread bags and jars are closed before teenagers begin.

Have the first people try to make their sandwiches. Team members can either remain silent or try to help using only words; they may not touch the supplies or the sandwich maker's hands. Call time after a minute, and let everyone see the results. Then have other students try, being sure the bags and jars are closed again for each new sandwich maker.

After everyone has had a turn trying to make a sandwich, gather everyone together. Read aloud Hebrews 12:2-3. Then ask:

• **How successful were you at making sandwiches when you weren't able to focus on the sandwiches themselves?**

• **How is that like trying to live as a Christian without focusing on Jesus?**

• **What things do we focus on besides Jesus?**

• **How does focusing on Jesus make a difference?**

• **What can you do to focus on Jesus?**

Feet-Tack-Toe

OVERVIEW: Teenagers will answer questions that review their understanding of the Bible and Jesus Christ.

TIME INVOLVED: 10 to 15 minutes

SUPPLIES: masking tape or sidewalk chalk (if you're playing outside), a washable marker, paper, pen, a Bible trivia game (optional)

PREPARATION: Prepare a list of questions and answers from recent lessons, or use questions from any type of Bible trivia game. Using the masking tape or sidewalk chalk, lay out a traditional tick-tack-toe board on the floor or sidewalk, approximately five feet across.

Have teenagers form teams of three or four. Place two teams at the tick-tack-toe board. Determine which team will be the X's and which team will be the O's. Have teenagers remove their shoes and socks. Using the washable marker, put X's or O's on top of each person's feet.

Begin play with the X team. Ask the first question. Give the team ten seconds to confer and answer the question. A correct response allows them to place an X (someone's feet) on the game board. If they answer incorrectly, share the correct answer. Then ask the O team the next question. Alternate questions between the teams. Continue play until a team gets three pairs of feet in a row—across, up and down, diagonally—or the game ends in a tie.

Encourage teamwork at all times to prevent one or two teenagers from being the sole answerers for their teams.

Like regular tick-tack-toe, this game can be addictive! Have plenty of questions ready. You and your group may be surprised at how much they know. Be flexible and alert for opportunities to explain or discuss some of the answers more deeply while teenagers play. Most of all, have fun!

The Bottomless Pit

OVERVIEW: Teenagers will work together to get over a "bottomless pit" and compare the pit to adversity in their lives.

TIME INVOLVED: 15 to 20 minutes

SUPPLIES: a Bible, two chairs, string, masking tape, and scissors

PREPARATION: Place the two chairs about six feet apart. Tie one end of a piece of string to each chair, about two feet off the ground. Tape two pieces of masking tape on the floor parallel to the string. Each piece of masking tape should be about three feet away from the string. Tape a third piece of masking tape to the floor directly below the string. (See the diagram on page 110.) The space between the chairs and the two pieces of masking tape is the "bottomless pit."

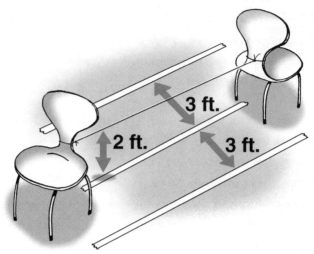

Have teenagers gather around the bottomless pit. Say: **In our jour-ney today, we've come to a bottomless pit! We have to get across this pit because we're trying to escape a cave that is home to a giant polar bear! The only way out of the cave is on the other side of the pit.** Explain that teenagers can't jump across because the opening is only two feet tall (the top is marked by the piece of string). If they put any weight on the floor between the two pieces of tape, they will "fall to their deaths." The piece of tape in the middle of the pit is a razor-sharp rock. Teenagers may balance their feet on the rock, but they can't use their hands on the rock, as it will cut off their hands. Explain that the challenge is for the entire group to get across the pit intact before the polar bear attacks.

Give the group several minutes to complete this challenge. When they're across the pit, have them sit down around the pit, and ask:

• **What was this exercise like for you? Explain.**

• **What was difficult about this exercise?**

• **What was the key to success?**

Read Romans 5:3-5 aloud, and ask:

• **What do you think this Scripture means?**

• **How is crossing the bottomless pit like facing suffering in our** own lives?

• **What experiences have you had with suffering?**

• **How have your experiences made you stronger?**

Listening to the Shepherd

OVERVIEW: One teenager will try to cross an obstacle course blindfolded with the help of the "shepherd's" voice.

TIME INVOLVED: 15 to 20 minutes

SUPPLIES: a Bible, a blindfold, various obstacles

PREPARATION: Set up an obstacle course in the playing area.

You'll need three volunteers: the Lost Lamb, the Shepherd, and the Wolf. The rest of the group will be Noise.

Blindfold the Lost Lamb, and explain to the group that the Lost Lamb needs to get from one side of the obstacle course to the other. The Shepherd's job is to guide the Lost Lamb across the room by giving him or her verbal directions. The Shepherd can move anywhere in the room to give directions, but can't get closer than six feet to the Lost Lamb. The Wolf's job is to distract and confuse the Lost Lamb. He or she can do this by giving false directions or drowning out the voice of the Shepherd. The Wolf can't move around the room but must stay near the opposite wall. The Noise group will talk, chat, and make general noise to provide more distraction. They can't talk directly to the Lost Lamb, and they must keep their noise at a normal conversational level.

Once students understand the game, have them begin. When the Lost Lamb has been safely guided to the other side of the playing area, have students switch roles and play again. Continue in this manner as long as time allows.

When you're finished playing, ask:

• **Lost Lambs, what was it like to have to try to listen to the Shepherd over all of the distractions?**

• **How did you cross the room safely?**

• **How difficult was it to trust the Shepherd's voice? Explain.**

• **How distracting were the other voices? Explain.**

• **Was the Wolf able to distract or confuse you in any way? Explain.**

Have students read John 10:7-18, and ask:

• How is this passage like the game we just experienced?

• If God were trying to speak to you in some way, how would you recognize the voice as God's?

• Who or what is the Wolf in your life?

• Who or what is Noise in your life?